# ATTUNED

## A PSYCHOLOGIST'S REFLECTIONS

# ATTUNED

*A Psychologist's Reflections*

*by*

Dr. Rashmi Pandey

*Pascal Editions*
*New York*

www.pascaleditions.com

LIBRARY OF CONGRESS CATALOGING-IN-PUBLICATION DATA:

Names: Pandey, Rashmi, [date] author.

Title: Attuned: A Psychologist's Reflections / Rashmi Pandey

Description: First Edition. | New York: Pascal Editions [2023]

Subjects: Psychology, Therapy, Memoir

ISBN: 978-0-9890855-9-5 [print]

1 3 5 7 9 10 8 6 4 2

First Edition

## Disclaimer

*Any opinions expressed in this document are those of the author, and do not necessarily reflect the views, policies or position of the publisher or of any agency or organization. With the exception of family and colleagues specifically named, the names, descriptions and characteristics of persons discussed in this book have been changed in order to honor and preserve client privacy. Incidents, personal histories and client-therapist conversations have also been changed.*

*Clients represented herein are not portraits of actually existing individuals. They are composite creations intended to illustrate and highlight specific therapeutic challenges clients commonly present, and to indicate common approaches to treatment.*

*In addition, opinions and information provided in this this book are intended for general purposes only and not as professional medical or therapeutic advice in specific cases. The author and publisher make no representations or warranties regarding the effectiveness or applicability of any information provided herein, and will not be held liable for any errors, omissions, or misinterpretations.*

*Neither author nor publisher are responsible for any actions taken based on the information provided in this book, and strongly advise readers to seek professional advice from qualified medical and/or therapeutic practitioners before taking any actions.*

*To My Parents*

# CONTENTS

*Acknowledgements*

*Preface*

# ACKNOWLEDGMENTS

Writing a storybook on my clinical experience as a psychologist has been an enriching journey. This creation wouldn't have been possible without an entire village of support and guidance at every step of my professional and personal journey.

First and foremost, I am immensely grateful to my clients, who have taught me resilience, humility, and empathy in my journey as a psychologist. I learned with them, and from their experiences, their pain and struggles, and I rejoiced their success and growth throughout the healing process. These are real people, in situational crises in which we all find ourselves at some point in our lives.

I wish to express my gratitude to several other inspirational sources who contributed to my personal and professional growth throughout my journey in becoming a clinical psychologist.

I wish to thank my Professor, Dr. La Don Jackson, who was also my doctoral thesis Chair, for being a continuing source of encouragement and guidance. His realistic and practical approach aided me in my selection of research work targeting immigration and acculturation.

Next, I am grateful for an excellent clinical training opportunity under the guidance of Dr. Richard Bolnick, Dr. John Jochem, and Dr. Susan Richardson, and for their support and encouragement throughout both my internship and my postdoctoral fellowship.

I especially wish to thank Dr. Bolnick for walking me through the steps of private practice. He continues to be there as my mentor and guide to this day.

My professional colleagues at various junctures of inpatient and outpatient work also continue to hold great value for me, for their continued presence, words of wisdom, guidance, and their long-lasting friendship.

I have been deeply gratified by my association and collaboration with the American Psychological Association as a researcher and as a presenter at various annual conferences, where I continue my learning process.

My goals as a clinician have been deeply inspired by the research and work of the world-renowned psychiatrist and "father of cognitive-behavioral therapy," Dr. Aaron Beck, and of his daughter, Dr. Judith Beck.

Also, my skills in empathy and understanding would not be what they are today without the client-centered approach of Carl Rogers.

My thoughts, ideas and reflections on my clinical experience would not have taken the form they have without my friend and editor, David, who brain-stormed and challenged me on each case and story line, providing brilliant input and support.

My final gratitude is towards my friends and family and three most important men in my life—my husband Yogendra with whom I built a home away from home in the United States and began the beautiful journey of my life and career as we explored the country, culture and people; and my sons, Gerv and Yash, who have been my cheerleaders, my readers and my finest critics during the creation of this book.

# PREFACE

Soon after I began writing the first few pages of this book, I found myself wondering about its readers. Who would they be? Why would they bother? Why would someone want to read a book of stories by a therapist?

I knew of course that millions of people *do* read books by therapists. Every public library, every college library, every Barnes and Noble, every book shop, even Walmart and Amazon, has a psychology or self-help section. On those shelves may sit a Freud and a Jung, a Skinner or a Frankl, Bettelheim or Beck, but alongside them there will be even more pop therapy bestsellers sporting an entire alphabet soup of letters—CBT, DBT, REBT, NLP. Each promise to help you lose weight, stay focused and 'be all you can be.'

The buyers of therapy books do more than just buy books on the subject. As reported by the web site statista.com, in 2021 some 41.7 million people "received mental health treatment or counseling in the past year." That number has gone up virtually each year for decades.

Clearly, there's an interest in therapy as such. But why read the thoughts and experiences of one particular therapist—myself?

Again, I could think of a few reasons. Someone considering getting therapy might want to know what sort of person they would be seeing, and what the actual process might be like. Reading about psychology in the abstract is one thing. Sitting down and admitting to fears and problems, to thoughts and feelings that you've never shared with anyone else your entire life, is something quite different.

Who will be that person? Will they understand? Empathize? Can they really help? What can you expect in therapy, and from therapy? A book could be like that initial conversation that introduces the patient to the therapist and the process.

A book like that could also help someone thinking about becoming a therapist themselves. Hearing an actual practitioner describe actual cases could illuminate the process in a way pure theory never could.

Then there are those actual cases themselves. Those can make for very interesting reading. The estranged couple that never stops arguing, the son or daughter in lifelong conflict with their parents, the drug or news or social media addict, the victim of depression, of anxiety, of trauma, of sexual confusion.

Every story is a mini-drama, and many of those stories are our own. Moreover, many have hopeful uplifting endings. Yes: it *is* possible to overcome one's fears, to get over past traumas, fall in love again and make it work. People do it all the time.

But how? A therapeutic case history can show you, detailing the passage step-by-step.

Most, unfortunately, don't.

Most psychological reports are normally written up in dry ghastly academic-sounding prose that cause depression all by themselves. Still, all the elements of literature and even entertainment are there—high drama, passionate conflict, mysteries, surprises, confrontations. A therapist sees all those things. I certainly have.

But as I found myself wondering about my possible readers, I also began wondering about me. Isn't that the essence of therapy—self-examination? Why was *I* writing? Why does any therapist write?

That was no mystery. A seed is planted, and the seed grows into a tree, and as time passes the branches of the tree breaks into leaves. So, with any thoughtful professional. You work in a particular area for long enough, and you begin to think about what you're seen and experienced, to articulate the way your journey has followed—and diverged from—the path on which you originally set out. We reflect on what we do, and we want to share those reflections.

But there was another reason too.

The classic areas of therapeutic need haven't changed. Trauma and anxiety, marital and parental dysfunction, obsession and addiction and sexual maladjustment, those are parts of the human condition that will always be with us. But some of the problems people face today—social media addiction, rapid and radical demographic change, over-medication with ever-novel drugs, ecological dread, rampant obesity, transgender surgery—these are new. New and different.

When I began my clinical studies, I did not for a moment think I would end up operating my own private practice. When I began that practice, I did not even remotely imagine that I would be helping clients grapple with the challenges they face now. Therapists trained to handle Oedipus Complexes that now officially no longer exist, now end up facing global pandemics, gender dysphoria, political hyperpolarization, omniphobia, Trump Derangement Syndrome. (*Is* that a syndrome, or just a meme? And what *is* a meme, anyway?)

This is not a complaint; it's an only an observation. But one of several that are ongoing themes in this book, and that I think therapeutic professionals and clients both will benefit from reading. Things have changed, and therapy can cushion and blunt the more destructive aspects of that change.

Therapy can help clients see the opportunities inside the challenges, the growth that can emerge from the struggle. Some of those struggles are part of the human condition, and some involve the new high-velocity technological condition that is revolutionizing daily life. A way to cope is needed, and is available, and is evolving. I wanted to express the value of that help, how it's often applied in real-life instances, and the new directions in which it is moving.

And so—here is my book. What have I put in it? Allow me to lay out a brief map for those about to travel its pages.

The first part is a short description of what got me interested in the clinical profession, the areas of psychology, and finally into practicing psychology. There is some relevant personal background, but very little: this is not an autobiography, but a presentation of what brought me to therapeutic practice, what I have seen there, and where I believe the profession is heading.

The core of the book presents ten paradigm cases—cases that stick in my mind, partly because of their own unique interest, and partly because of what they say about the particular problem each one addresses. Each standalone chapter has a particular focus—obesity, addiction, couples therapy, social adjustment, and so on.

You can read them in any order, and together I believe they present a fair spectrum of the sort of situations and issues with which a practitioner deals.

These ten cases are not exhaustive, of course; for human individuality can never be exhausted. But I would be surprised if the reader cannot find something of his own challenges in the problems of these clients, and perhaps something of a way to successfully handle them, as the clients I have helped have.

The concluding section contains a few of my reflections on therapy, the vocation of being a therapist, and the 'brave new world' that both clients and therapists are having to face. Changes are coming thick and fast, and what exactly is it that is coming? No one really knows.

But some things will persist, too. Empathy. Connection. An attunement. Forgiveness and self-forgiveness.

The power of therapy.

## CHAPTER ONE

# RESURRECTION

It was a sudden decision during lunch. An impulse.

I went to the PHP floor and asked for Mrs. Smith. PHP stands for 'Partial Hospitalization.' It's a program used to treat people suffering from mental illness and substance abuse. In partial hospitalization, the patient continues to live at home, but commits to visiting a treatment center up to seven days a week.

Mrs. Smith was a nurse always being rotated across multiple psych floors. I never failed to see her when I visited the PHP, and when I stopped in that day, there she was, as always, handling a report.

She looked up, saw me, and looked away.

"Mrs. Smith, how are you?"

"Hi, Dr. Pandey."

"How are things going?"

She closed her report.

"I was wondering if I could see Martha." I asked. "She was discharged from upstairs last week for PHP. I'd like to—."

"Martha's dead."

She opened another one.

"She killed herself."

"She—?"

"She overdosed on pills last night. Took the whole bottle."

Mrs. Smith made a note in the new report. This was nothing new. She'd seen it before. People die. There are always new reports to be filed. She had no time to go into details with rookie medical practitioners, much less comfort them. She got back to work.

I walked away, slowly, then more rapidly.

*It's my fault. My fault.* The words seared through my head. *I'm to blame,* I told myself. *She should have stayed as an inpatient under observation. I should have fought for her. I should have fought for her to stay inpatient.*

I began running. My tears began running too, running down my cheeks.

*If only I had fought for her, if only I had fought for her harder. I could have reached her. I could have saved her...*

*But I couldn't save her, not now. Martha was dead.*

I didn't know it at the time, but so was my career; my career, and my future as a hospital-based clinical psychologist.

*I could have reached her. I could have saved her...*

But it was too late, too late. Everything had come to an end for Martha.

And for me? I had arrived at the beginning.

Martha would tell me that as she looked outside the window of her tiny hospital room, she could see figures floating in the air, drifting towards her. Some had terrifying faces, like hungry wild animals. Some had no faces, only hues and shapes, no features other than an abyss. They horrified her. She would scream and run to the door.

"*Help me,*" she would scream, "*they're coming for me... please, someone... they're going to kill me... rape me... oh my God!*"

She would clutch her rosary, and start to jump up and down to shake their hands, their mouths, their fangs, off her tear-stained hospital gown. Her shrieks were blood-curdling. It was as if crowds of demons were engulfing her, stabbing her with many sharp knives.

There was an incident during her inpatient stay when the ward nurse had momentarily stepped out for a drink of water when she heard Martha's screams. She sprinted back to the room and tried to hold her, comfort her, shush her and get her to calm down.

But Martha was out of control. She pushed the nurse to the wall and leaped into the hallway and ran towards the locked door at the end, and when the door wouldn't open, she would bang her head on it in a frenzy, over and over and over, simultaneously screaming and praying

Sometimes the nurse could bring her back to her room. Sometimes it took several nurses, or people from Security. Eventually Martha would be sedated, and afterwards the nurse would make an entry onto a form or into a database. Patient Martha had experienced another episode.

Mental illnesses are like physical ones. There are afflictions that are inconvenient and unpleasant, but light, and treatable. There are other afflictions that are agonizing, incapacitating, and in some cases fatal. Paranoid schizophrenia is one of the most serious psychiatric disorders. It severely distorts the way we think, behave, express emotions, perceive reality, and connect with others. This condition affects more than one percent of the world population. It is not yet curable, and may never be, although the search for a cure never ends. The symptoms are usually managed with antipsychotic medication and therapy.

Martha was admitted to a Chicago psychiatric hospital when she tried to wash her body with bleach. Why, asked the attending physician brought in to seeing her. She felt 'dirty,' she said. She had been raped, she said. She had been raped by a demon. The demon had overpowered her. The demon had wanted her to write a letter full of profanities and post it to her church. She refused, and the demon had made her pay the price.

Martha was 68 years old. She was a widow with two grown-up daughters; a former elementary school teacher, now retired. She was a believing Christian, and read the Bible devoutly, volunteering at her local church as a Bible study teacher.

Martha was small in stature—a tiny, petite woman. She had the kindest face and a genuine smile. Her eyes had a touch of sadness—a loneliness, no doubt stemming of the recent death of her husband owing to lung cancer after three long years of battle and many surgeries. They had been together for almost forty-five years.

A year before being herself committed, he had passed away and she had lost him. And sometimes during the course of that year, she lost her mind as well.

Martha was my very first paranoid schizophrenic. Yes, I know how silly that sounds, and even how cold—like comparing a person's psychological tragedy to one's first bicycle. The fact remains, she was one of my very first patients of any sort as I began my duties as a Licensed Clinician at the Chicago hospital where I first began my professional career, and I wanted *passionately* to do well, help others, heal the sick. I was as idealistic as a young doctor could possibly be, and Martha was as sweet an older person as an older person could possibly be, almost like the ideal, gentle, slightly old-fashioned mother we would all like to have. You wanted to hug her. Sometimes I did!

And if that sounds a little excessive—well, perhaps it's time that I introduce myself in more detail.

This book is about therapy, not about me. I want to share what I've learned about a process very valuable to the health of our society, very important to our collective futures, and perhaps very important to you the individual—you the reader. That doesn't involve dwelling on my personal likes and dislikes, my personal relation-ships, or much of my personal history, and I don't plan to

Except where relevant. And it's relevant here. But I'll be brief.

I was not born in Chicago. I was born in India. I was very fortunate to be born in India, fortunate to be born into a wonderful family there, and especially fortunate to be have a father who could not have been more loving or supportive.

In Indian culture there is a tendency for parents to concentrate all their attention on the future success of the sons, and to subtly and not-so-subtly edge the daughters into a future as wives and mothers. That was never my father's view. If I wanted that as my future, fine. But he was ready to help me do whatever I wanted, to see me rise as high as I wished, and to take wing in whatever direction I pleased.

As far back as I can recall I knew what that direction was: I wanted to be a doctor, a helper, a healer.

Why? I don't really know. Why do birds fly? It's in their nature. It was in my nature from childhood to want to help others, and not only those suffering physical injury, but those suffering *inwardly*; those in emotional pain.

Perhaps it had something to do with the unspoken spiritual mindset of an Indian heritage— that long history of mystics and gurus, Hindu philosophers and Buddhist monks, with their consensus that suffering and liberation comes from within, that only by looking within could we ever find a way out. Whatever it was, I soon found myself drifting into the medical field, and then focusing on its psychological areas, and then training in behavioral medicine.

The studies were long, and the best places to study were far away. English-speaking schools and institutions were the world leaders at the time, but English was not a problem. English is not so much a second language as a first language as far as Indian intellectual life is concerned. I was easily fluent enough to pass the necessary exams, and so I began my clinical training at the University of Sydney in Australia.

Marriage and family responsibilities made the remainder of my clinical training quite the story! It took yet another turn when my quest for doctoral education and research required moving to Chicago in the United States.

But move I did: it was my calling, something I felt I had been made for.

The moves were valuable, not just educationally but intellectually. Emigrating showed me a good deal about the challenges, psychological as well as practical, of the immigrant. Eventually it became the subject of my graduate thesis, and gave me a deepened under-standing of immigration as a growing therapeutic need.

But—it was also *fun!* The novelty. New people, new ideas, new sights, new worlds. I *loved* being a student. The hours were impossible, the amount we needed to learn immense—and yet, the students in my classes and study groups were a delight, hilarious and ridiculous college capers never stopped happening, I made friends who will stay my friends for the rest of my life, and the books and lectures and knowledge I was exposed to was endlessly enriching and fascinating.

I loved it. And when after graduation I was finally hired and posted to a major medical institution in Chicago to practice what I had learned, I was in ecstasy.

But not for very long.

This isn't a book about the failures and challenges of institutional American healthcare. If it were, it would be a very thick book. Suffice it to say that I entered the hospital system with every intention of using all that I had learned to help and heal suffering patients. I soon found the reality of hospital care to be very different. Facilities were over-crowded, services were understaffed, paperwork and regulations seemed almost infinite, and the universal assumption seemed to be was that every problem had a pharmacological solution, and that solution always came first, not because it worked, but because it gave a quick measurable result. People entering a hospital environment were treated the way automobiles are treated at garages: they were there to get a quick fix and be put back on the road at once.

It was an efficient enough approach, sometimes, for simple physical ailments. But if the patient's problem was *not* immediately material? If the problem was a broken spirit and not merely a broken bone?

That didn't matter. The goal was always the same: do something to make the person appear a little better, then push them out of the examination room or hospital bed and back on the street as fast as possible.

The method of choice was always the same, too. Drugs. The default response to everything was to prescribe drugs. Drugs worked. They produced an immediate, sought-for response: they shut the patient up. Pain and suffering went away. Or at least seemed too. So too, often, did agency and emotion, but that was an acceptable price to pay— or rather, for patients to pay.

Admittedly, psychologists in search of deeper and more comprehensive approaches to healing had more than just institutional pressures to face. There was the whole vast problem of method. I had a felt certainty that a more profound way of working with patients was needed—a way that addressed the whole person, that was more than just a gateway to lifelong drug dependency.

But what? Naturally I looked to psychotherapy, but at the time shopping among the various psychotherapies was like being a child in the world's largest toy shop. The shop had everything!

All the psychoanalytic and psychodynamic therapies were still there—Freud and Freudians and Jung and Jungians and Reich and dozens of others. Powerful as it was, behavior therapy had never quite taken off, but its offshoots were everywhere, an explosion of alphabet soup—CBT and REBT and DBT and NLP and so on. There were rather fringe movements like Gestalt and Primal

Scream and Ericksonian hypnosis and Past-Life Therapy and whatnot. Each claimed to work. Each *did* work, in their own way, to a certain degree, depending on the patient. Which to choose?

In the end, a consensus had begun to emerge. The psychodynamic therapies seemed to be fading away, and the more cognitively flavored of the behavioral therapies seemed to be on the rise. I became aware that Cognitive-Behavioral Therapy was increasingly the therapeutic default favored by hospitals. Rightly so: it was effective, clear, systemic and produced quick and measurable positive results. That was also its main drawback: it produced the same sort of quick shallow measurable improvement that was needed for a medical institution to send one patient quickly out the door so as to make room for the next billable customer.

Everywhere in modern hospital healthcare, I saw quantity trump quality. And yet I remained. For the fact was, the cognitive and behavioral approaches used in such setting might not be perfect in every way, but very often they *were* effective. They *did* produce improvements. Those improvements *were* quick and they *were* measurable. What was wrong with that? Nothing.

Except that there were problems and patients who required more than an antidepressant and some homework assignments. Much more.

Martha was such a patient. Such a person. She was not simply troubled or conflicted or depressed. She was insane. That is not a technical term we use in the profession any longer—diagnoses are much more specific, and less judgmental.

But a few words with Martha soon made you see that she was seriously, tragically, disturbed. She heard voices, and the voices "were in her head," and they were the voices of demons. She was a plaything of these devils. She told me she was constantly being persecuted and injured by them. Physically injured: her body was mis-handled and tortured by these demonic entities in all kinds of brutal and sexual ways. These entities were 'soul murderers.' They were using her, harming her, coercing and in all sorts of despicable ways. They could attack her suddenly, at any time, without any reason, she believed. They were tricksters: they could even make themselves look like normal people, even friends, and so Martha would often keep others at a distance, falling into paranoia and distrust. We doctors—we could be demons too.

I wasn't aware of all this at first. As a Medicare provider, I was allowed to see older patients on the unit. I met Martha in the patient community area. There, patients not considered dangerous could sit and engage in harmless activities, and while Martha's ideas were crazy, she herself was small, motherly, soft-spoken, well-mannered, kind. She suffered within, but nothing about her suggested that she would harm others. She was pointed out to me by a staffer, I watched her, and I liked what I could see of her very much; there was a kind of radiance coming from Martha that touched me. She seemed so close to living in the everyday world peacefully and happily. Surely it wouldn't take much to restore to that world, I thought. I'm sorry to say that at the time I had a somewhat inflated sense of what could be done in such situations. My optimism in those early years was immense. She seemed *so close* to being well. Surely with just a *little* kindness and understanding, with just a little help...

That's the kind of *hubris* that, in the world of mental health, can end tragically. And did.

But I was not thinking like that the first time I saw her. I simply walked up and introduced myself.

"Hello Mrs. Franklin," I said. "I'm Dr. Pandey, a new psychologist on the unit."

"Well, how do you do, young lady. It's so nice to meet you."

"And you."

"Please, call me Martha," she said.

"Are you having a nice day today, Martha?"

"I suppose so."

It was September and we could see from the window several patients accompanied by aides strolling outside along in the large hospital compound. There were trees, grass, space. Martha looked at it all with a yearning.

Martha took a chair with a folded blanket on it. She wore a thin hospital gown and she wrapped the large blanket around her petite body. It engulfed her tiny frame.

She called me to sit next to her. I pulled up a chair.

I was not naïve. I had already looked at her chart to familiarize myself with her condition, her meds, the comments of those who had examined her. She was diagnosed with Paranoid Schizophrenia, with a secondary diagnosis of bipolar disorder. She had twice attempted to break away from the floor. She'd been injected with Haldol to control that at-risk behavior. Was she a danger to others? There were no such indications yet. Nonetheless I stayed fully aware of the nurses' station close by.

She gazed out the window. "Look at that blue sky," she said.

She sighed.

"They won't let me go outside, you know," she said

Her eyes were sad as they looked intently and plaintively at me.

"You see, Doc," she whispered, leaning closer as though including me in her confidence, "I'm nuts."

She said it so sweetly I couldn't help but smile. "You seem very well to me, Martha. I'm sure that, even if you do seem to be having problems, you'll recover soon."

She shook her head sadly.

"No," she said, "the voices just won't stop. They just won't let me alone."

"The voices?"

She nodded.

"Whose voices, Martha?"

"*Demons*," she whispered.

She put two fists to the sides of her head and shot her index fingers up. Horns!

"Sometimes it's The Devil himself!" she said. "But usually it's other devils. All sorts of devils. Crowds of devils. All yelling and screaming and swearing at me."

"What do they say to you?"

"Terrible things. Obscene things. Their mouths are just filthy. Filthy!"

"I'm so sorry to hear that, Martha. They don't do that all the time, do they?"

"No," she admitted. "Sometimes they do go away... but at other times, they're loud, Doctor, so loud, so loud you wouldn't believe it. So *loud*, so *angry*. They want to *break through*."

"Break through how?"

"Break through *here*. Into our world. And they do! They do. At night. Sometimes at night they break through."

"What happens then?"

"They break the walls and the doors. They shake my bed. And they hurt me," she said. "They *hurt* me."

She began to cry.

I tried to change the subject. I had come in to introduce myself, not to start a line of conversation that would upset her. She was very open to that. Soon we were talking small talk. Martha began chatting and laughing. So did I. We were getting on famously.

The nurses' station noticed. A report soon reached her attending physician, whom I will call 'Dr. Crawford.' I found myself officially assigned to attend to her.

I had not been put in charge of her case in any formal charge sense. Other practitioners were, and they were the ones who prescribed her medication and directed her overall treatment. I was simply there to observe and assist.

But Martha took to me. And vice versa. And in hospital settings, where everything is about maintaining the status quo, about nothing happening, about reducing possible 'incidents,' that kind of connection matters. My presence might lift her spirits, it might calm her—it might reduce the likelihood of an 'incident.'

It was an assignment I relished. Incidents? There was not a one. Most of the time Martha seemed to me quite normal. If 'normal' described the behavior of some of the doctors and staff, Martha was better than normal—she was fun to talk to, pleasant, engaging. I came to like her, even to admire her.

I knew about the foul language and the brutality of the hallucinations she described experiencing. But her stance towards them was not cowardly or pitiable. She seemed a rather brave and strong person bearing up remarkably well. She believed in demons and The Devil, but also angels and God.

For Martha, beyond the darkness lay an underlying light; perhaps that was the source of her radiance--her moments of genuine happiness.

But her fight was a losing battle. The demons were becoming stronger, she confessed to me one day. Stronger, ever stronger. The demons were 'breaking through.' They were no longer satisfied with just abusing her body, no. More and more, she said, they were trying to break through into *her mind*. They were trying to possess *her*. And it terrified her.

And, more and more, what terrified Martha was beginning to depress and frustrate me as well. It wasn't that I believed in her demons. It was that, institutionally and in every other way, I could do nothing to help.

I'd entered the psychological profession to help others. But the longer I worked in a hospital psychiatric setting, the more I found myself facing not just an institutional culture more concerned with avoiding 'incidents' and dispensing drugs, but facing people with conditions that just would not respond to any treatment whatever.

It was not a matter administering a cure. There *were* no cures. We could act as though we were making a difference. But really, we were only going through the motions. There was nothing a practitioner could do but stand there and watch them suffer. We were not doctors. We were jailers.

Yet that—for the most part—is an over-statement. Yes, we tried to give the people the system had sequestered as pleasant an atmosphere as we could. We tried to present such distractions and alleviations as we could. In cases like myself and Martha, we could even provide genuine friendship and affection, though we were frequently reminded of the need to keep a professional distance.

But we weren't exorcists. We couldn't *dispel demons*. We could not dissolve illusions, wave away hallucinations, resolve irresolvable neurological medical conditions.

The effect of that professional impotence on my colleagues and peers was corrosive. They were like me: they could try to make the patient as comfortable as possible, but that was all they could do. In many cases—in most, it seemed—there was no healing and no progress: only medication and more medication. I found myself working with colleagues who had given up on such patients entirely. Their entire professional function was to drug the patients so thoroughly that they no longer gave staff and practitioners any trouble, to reduce intractable patients into easily handled vegetables. And if the patients drifted through the days mindlessly, shadows of the living persons they once had been? That was fine.

In Charles Dickens' *A Christmas Carol*, there's a scene in which the ghost of Jacob Marley, draped in chains, is howling with sorrow in the afterlife because he can witness human suffering but no longer do something about it.

My situation was not so over-dramatic, but at times I was not that far from Marley's despair. I could see myself following the path of too many of the staff and residents, and slipping into decades of cold indifference, agreeing with pushing drugs into anonymous veins with as little concern as a street pusher.

Some patients literally did not know I was there, and even with the bright and pleasant ones, like Martha, my skills and training were almost beside the point. My conversations with Martha might provide her brief islands of peace, but they could not keep her demons at bay, and when her attending physician pumped her with sufficient doses of anti-psychotics, what was the point in talking? There was no one there to hear.

I continued my regular briefings with 'Dr. Crawford.' They had become more and more frustrating. They would last no more than a few minutes. He would invariably cut my comments short with a robotic statement such as, "She's a gone case of psychosis. There's nothing we can do. Best practice is to stabilize her enough with anti-psychotics to get her out of here and open up some more unit space. See if we can step her down to PHP (the Partial Hospitalization program) and move her out."

My talks with Martha became more and more poignant for us both. It hurt me to see her taken away to be over-medicated for the hundredth time and shut away into a blank room till our next talk. At times I felt her reaching out for a talk with me like a person gasping for oxygen. It was an asphyxiation I came to share. Slowly she was corroding here, and one day I asked myself: was I corroding here too?

It was a rude awakening to have at the very beginning of my career as an inpatient clinician. I began to wonder. *Was* this the right career path for me. Most of my colleagues would kill for this job and its excellent perks, let alone the brand prestige of being associated with one of the world's top teaching hospitals.

But what else would I do? Where else should I go?

Laypersons have a very poor understanding of mental illness. They imagine the label describes a particular condition, when in fact it covers a wide spectrum of conditions.

At one end are people afflicted with literal brain damage—serious neurological malfunction so severe that restoration to health is simply not an option. All that can be done is to give them all the comfort one can.

At the opposite extreme are people in perfect physical health who function well enough, but who have some deeply disturbing personal dissatisfaction they wish to overcome. Grief, poor impulse control, obsessive inclinations, anger issues.

In some cases, a psychologist may encounter people who aren't ill or suffering in any way at all, but still crave psychological change. They want to be *more* focused, *more* productive—better versions of themselves.

But most everyone falls somewhere in the middle. We live our lives well enough, but keep revisiting painful memories, don't always focus easily or reason clearly, act in ways that are self-destructive, wish we had greater motivation or better social skills.

And that's fortunate! Because nearly all such 'conditions' can be addressed and be improved. Thoughts and feelings *can* be examined and be modified, and because of that, most people experiencing subjective problems can be helped, at least to some degree.

But some can't.

Sometimes medicine and therapy encounters people who, for reasons that are hard, chemical, neurological, cannot be helped at all. Sometimes their suffering can be chemically or surgically alleviated, but that is all that we can (at this point) do.

This isn't to say that patients unreachable by treatment should be abandoned or neglected. Far from it. Comforting and caring for such patients is a high calling all by itself. Many caregivers in such institutions do indeed have high compassion, and should rightly be honored.

But in the institution to which I had come, I could see that compassion eroding all around me. Slowly the temptation to use medication as the one-stop solution to every problem was becoming engrained. Patient after patient would be medicated into a drugged stupor. End of story.

Few people realize how many forms of mental suffering *can* be lightened and even completely cured. Many still have a picture in their mind of the classic Freudian patient lying on the couch for thirty years discussing his or her mother, and remaining as neurotic as ever. This picture is false. Highly effective therapies have come into being— Behavior Therapy, Cognitive-Behavior Therapy, Rational-Behavior Therapy, Dialectical Therapy, Reality Therapy, Brief Therapy, Reality Therapy. All of them abound in studies showing effectiveness in solving client complaints.

This is what I had seen myself doing. I knew that depression, anxiety, guilt, self-limiting behaviors could be addressed and reduced, and I felt that that was my purpose, my calling as a practitioner. I wanted to make a difference to someone.

Yet I'd put myself in a situation where I made virtually no difference, and could not make a difference.

It bothered me deeply. Yes, I realized that medication and restraints were unavoidable in some cases. But not all. Not, I especially came to think, in the case of Martha.

Film director Orson Welles liked to tell a story about an uncle of his. The Uncle was a successful businessman, a family man. Well-liked, decent, pleasant. He only had one quirk. He thought every day was Christmas.

His friends regarded that belief as crazy. It was! But it was only one crazy belief in the context of hundreds of other sane and acceptable ones, and in every other respect the man seemed competent and responsible and engaging.

So... everybody shrugged, accepted the man as he was, and went on about their business.

As time went on, that was how I began to feel about Martha. When she described her voices and the demons molesting her at night, it could be quite off-putting. But she didn't dwell on that subject very often. Usually her conversation was friendly, charming, entertaining. She was pleasant company. Fun to talk to!

Did this sweet, tiny lady really need to be institutionalized, regularly injected with numbing antipsychotics, locked away in a facility built to house violent madmen? I came to wonder if Martha had been shunted away into a hospital simply because, like so many others here, no one wanted to bother with her.

But as my frustration grew, so did a realistic sense of my position. I was not happy where I was. I didn't feel effective doing what I was doing. I was probably deluding myself to be a good clinician. I certainly was not effective in giving Martha the extra attention I felt she needed. She was not *only* an assignment given to me by those in charge. I *cared* about her. But there was little I could do about it. Her voices and hallucinations went on as before, and her fears of demonic possession kept growing.

We would discuss Martha's plan of care regularly during the staff meeting twice a week. After her third week as an inpatient, 'Dr. Crawford' hinted that he would be stepping Martha down to the Partial Hospitalized Program. Martha would stay the entire day at the hospital, and go home for the night.

I wasn't sure if she was ready for this transition. After all, the 'demons' visited her most often at night, in the dark. Was that the best time for her to be alone? But I had no say. I was expected to help 'manage' her daily mood in the Day Room. Nothing more.

The following week, on my Monday morning rounds, that's what I did. I visited Martha in the Day Room. Other patients were there, some sitting silent and isolated, some with aides present, others half asleep. Martha was sitting by the window in her favorite spot, reading a book.

I greeted her. "Hi, Martha!"

"Hello, dear." She smiled and closed her book, eager to talk. "My, you are a sight for sore eyes!"

I sat next to her with my folder. I could see her trying to be her old, bright-spirited self. But something was wrong. I could read it in her posture, her expression. It lay on her, like a heavy weight.

We spoke for a few moments. I asked a question and she failed to respond. I asked several more. There was no answer. I thought I must have come after she'd been given her meds. Likely they'd dimmed her consciousness to the point that she was no longer aware of my presence.

I was sorry. Our talks had come to mean a great deal to me. But there was nothing I could do.

I prepared to stand up.

"Martha," I said, gently, "I have to go now. Be well, all right?"

I reached out to touch her arm.

"I'll come back to visit you again soon, dear, I promise—"

I touched her arm.

She *shrieked*, and *hurled* herself at me, her nails reaching like cats' claws for my eyes.

I threw up my arms, and her *scream* reverberated through the Day Room. It was more like the howl of some creature out of Hell than something human. We both went down, falling to the floor, and she roared and howled and began slashing at me.

I heard another scream.

It was mine.

Two guards stationed in the room were on top of her in moments.

They tried to pull her away.

She twisted and struggled.

Shocked, I looked into her face. The dear grandmotherly expression I found so touching was gone. Her eyes bulged and rolled; her skin was blotched, veins stood out in her forehead; flecks of spittle flew from her lips. The screaming *would not stop*. Her voice was no longer the gentle quiet voice I knew. It *felt* demonic: a cursing and a crying and a screaming all at once.

The guards finally managed to pull her away. I lay there shocked. I'd never seen such a trans-formation in my entire life.

I am a psychologist, a woman of science and medicine. I do not believe in demons or devils. I don't believe in demonic possession.

But that instant, just for a moment, I believed. I believed completely.

A nurse ran over and helped me get to my feet. Another one approached the two guards and tried to help them get Martha under control. The three of them barely managed to keep her restrained.

I rose, stunned and shaken.

The incident followed the formula that such incidents do. Drugs were administered. Martha grew passive, then unconscious. Staff arrived to calm the other patients in the room down. Martha was placed under restraints, and was sequestered. I was taken to see a nurse, then given several pieces of paperwork to sign, then unofficially interviewed, then scheduled for an official interview, then told I could go home.

I went home. Stunned.

After two days of observation and isolation, Martha was 'normal' again, normal and even upbeat. She saw me in by the nurse's station, and when I saw her approaching, I'm ashamed to say that I flinched. But I controlled myself. I smiled at her. A genuine smile. It was good to see her as Martha again, and not as whatever she had momentarily become two days earlier.

She came closer. She was tearful and looked down.

"I am so sorry—*so* sorry—for attacking you the other day."

"It's okay, Martha."

"No... No, it is *not* OK. And it wasn't me! *He* was here. *He* made me lunge at you. I would never do anything like that. I would never forgive myself for something like that. You're... you're like my daughter."

She was sobbing. She folded her hands in prayer.

I kept thinking about her for the rest of that day. I couldn't concentrate on any other patient. When I closed my eyes, I could see the tears on her cheeks, hear her sobbing.

I felt like screaming and crying out loud... Anger and guilt overwhelmed me.

When I left for the day, I felt lifeless, exhausted, done. I wanted to go home and sink into bed and into blank empty sleep.

I couldn't stop thinking about Martha. What next? What would they do to her now? She was so sorry, so tiny, so helpless, so alone, so in pain. What would happen to her?

I walked to the unit the next day and looked over at the PHP chart to see the section for the day programs. There was Martha's name. She was being transitioned out. The incident had made no difference.

I turned and went immediately to see 'Dr. Crawford.' He was standing at the nurses' station.

"Doctor," I said. "I've just seen the PHP chart. Do you really think Martha's recovered enough to be sent home evenings? I mean, after the incident in the Day Room—."

He actually laughed. "Doctor, she'll be hallucinating for the rest of her life. She's been on too many neuroleptics for too long. Do we really need her around here 24/7, causing problems like the one two days ago?" He shrugged. "She's as recovered as she's ever going to be. "Learn to live with it."

I was speechless. And yet, what was there for me to add?

I went to Martha's room and met her for the last time as an inpatient.

She didn't want to go. "I'm not well," she said. "I'm really not well. I know that. But if I don't go along with this, my daughters will send me to a nursing home. I can't go there. I wouldn't let John go to the nursing home. I took care of him at home till the very end."

"Dr. Pandey, even if I'm at PHP, please visit me. Promise you'll visit me."

"I will," I said. "I promise." I assured her that I would.

I didn't keep that promise. I stayed away from visiting her at PHP for the next few days. I didn't want my presence to trigger another violent reaction from Martha. Maybe my presence wasn't the cause, but I wasn't sure about many things any longer, including my diagnostic ability. How could I have missed the violence simmering so intensely under Martha's kindly surface? I missed it because I *liked* her—and so I'd allowed myself to lose my sense of objectivity and distance. Could I have seen her outburst emerging? Could I have kept it from happening? Was I to blame?

Yes or no, I had to see her again. If nothing else, just to reassure her that I was all right and was still her friend.

But I didn't. I didn't keep my promise, not to her, not to myself. I couldn't. The next time I dropped into the PHP floor to see Martha, Nurse Smith told me Martha had taken all her medications the night, and all at once.

She was quite dead.

The days and weeks that followed were hard. I gave a good deal of thought to my choice of a career. Even to whether I should continue at all. In therapy we're always telling our client to accept reality, to deal with the situation as it is, to forgive oneself and move on. How easy to say, how hard to do!

I was unable to move on. Her death put my entire future in question. I had failed a person I regarded as being under my care. And now she had taken her own life. Why stay in a profession where I could stumble so badly?

Therapy—the self-therapy of soberly facing reality—helped me center myself again.

No, I told myself, I had no reason to believe that I could have stopped Martha from eventually taking her own life. Her condition, in no small part, was a matter of brain chemistry that no known treatment could heal. She lived a life that, for her, was a constant barrage of rape by demons, an incessant intrusion of obscene demonic voices, a deepening fear of Satanic possession and the loss of one's eternal soul. It was not a happy life, nor a tolerable one. Maybe Martha imagined that by taking her life she was saving it on some religious level. I don't know. I do know that it was arrogant of me to think that my occasional company and conversations could have stopped it. She simply had too much to bear.

I tried very hard to reach her, and to support her, but in the end, she collapsed under that burden. I had no reason to think that anything I did could have stopped what ultimately happened.

But at least I did not fail to try. I knew that my all-too-brief presence in her life did indeed matter to her, and made a positive difference to her. If that is a small consolation, at least it is a real one. In small but genuine ways, her life was changed for the better by the fact that I was there.

And my life was changed by her, too, in ways that were not small at all. The end of her life was the end of my career as a hospital clinician.

It was not an overnight decision. After Martha I sat back and tried to look at my situation objectively. In hospital service, I would be assigned to caring for people I could not possibly help. Many suffered from conditions for which there was no remedy. I would not be in control of the patient's care: hospital policies and senior physicians would tell me what sort of care to provide and how and if—as with Martha—I disagreed, it would make no difference. I would have to stand by as nurses administered drugs as directed to keep troublesome people quiet.

I wanted to do more. I was eager to gain experience in a high-pressured inpatient environment involving crisis management. There were many benefits, such as interaction with and learning from highly skilled physicians and psychiatrists and becoming familiar with the entire team approach.... but I was craving a "talk therapy" to bring out the change that was unavailable to my chronic mentally ill patients with severe psychosis.

Where else could I go? How else could I fulfill that calling?

Over the years, the journey transformed a rookie psychologist in an inpatient setting to an established private practitioner and it certainly took time to get here. However, I now have my answer to, "but I wanted to do more".

I was fortunate to be trained by excellent clinicians during my internship and post-doctoral fellowship, and one of them still has an immense impact on my career. Dr. Richard Bolnick! He was my supervisor during internship rotation at St. Therese Medical Center, and over the years, he's become my guiding light.

It was Dr. Bolnick who walked me through the initial steps of beginning my own practice. He coached me about credentialing through private insurance companies, marketing my practice, and developing a keen sense of patience as I went along the ride of being a practicing clinician. I often model his empathic style.

I continued my inpatient work as I carefully made the transition into becoming a full-time clinical psychologist in a private practice. Soon that practice, Chicago Psychological, was born, and I was at the threshold of a new plateau in my career. I continued as a presence on staff, and I continue to maintain hospital affiliations and to expand my area of expertise through lectures, research, and psychology conferences.

But something more than that had happened—I had arrived at my calling, my *Ikigai*: the Japanese word for one's purpose in life, one's reason for being.

Private practice has proved to be the best career imaginable for me. I work with people I believe I *can* help, and I see them improve right before my eyes. Every clinician has their own therapeutic flare. Over the years I developed an integrative approach to mental health. At times direct and challenging towards my client but always mindful of being in their shoes.

I seldom miss my institutional life as a clinician. But even now, when I occasionally visit inpatient psych to check in with my patients, the memories come back; and Martha too. I was haunted by her memory for a long while. I'm still haunted by her. I can still see her face, hear her voice. I still think of her.

It's not the visit of a ghost or a demon. Far from it. It's the visit of a memory of a wonderful person, a memory that continues to shape and inspire my career and my practice.

No one has made clearer to me the importance of therapeutic care, or what can happen when that care fails. No one has made me realize more the importance of doing one's best, of seeing things rightly and not losing one's objectivity. No one taught me more about humility—about facing the tragic limitations of the therapist's profession.

All doctors lose patients, and not all patients can be saved. That is a given, a wall we cannot surmount.

But many *can* be saved. Martha's loss, so personally painful, also highlighted for me how very valuable a therapeutic success can be. I've seen patients with suicidal tendencies since then. I've helped them surmount that dark temptation, and seen them restored, affirming life throughout all its highs and lows. I rose out of the ashes of her death into a resurrection that made me a much more committed, much more determined, care-giver. A better clinician.

For that—and much else—I have Martha to thank.

CHAPTER TWO

# MODEL MINORITY

Among my clients, Reena holds a very special place. She was my very first client from an Indian immigrant family. She came from the same sort of background, the same culture, as I myself. I knew the social environment in which she moved, and the pressures to which she was subjected.

I was more fortunate than Reena; my parents were more sensitive and supportive. But with a different set of parents, or a different extended family, I could very well have ended up in the same difficult place.

That said, we understood one nonetheless another in a way unique to Indian women navigating the curious waters of American culture, and the even more complicated world of the Indian Diaspora in the Land of the Free.

In America there is a myth called 'the model minority.' It refers to members of minorities who are not only successful in terms of such classic American criteria as wealth, status, professional stature and other social indicators, but who embody higher personal standards as well, stricter standards of social and personal morality. This group demands that its members be better, finer, more accomplished than the American norm. It is not enough merely to shine: one must outshine others, outperform, over-deliver, always take the highest prize. In such communities there is no second place.

And if members of that community meet a high standard, but not the *very highest* standard? Then they're embarrassments. Failures. Trash. They've disgraced their family, their friends, the entire Indian community.

Nowadays Asian Indians and Southeast Asians are particularly expected to live out these myths and stereotypes before one another and before the general public. And sometimes this myth has its virtues: it may serve to inspire greater efforts, loftier ambitions.

But it can also foster the lie that any member of the model minority can reach the topmost heights of democratic society if he or she only works hard and relentlessly enough, never experiencing any difficulties in that aggressive demanding process.

This lie may compel members to deny very real personal problems, such as alcoholism, bipolar depression, suicidal tendencies and domestic violence. It can mask the worst sorts of coercion and cruelty while covering the surface with a varnish of All-American success, a vindication that is always monetary in an America where success is measured by excess.

It can even generate its own egocentric xenophobia, aggravating a competition that pits one minority group against another, or even against the majority. For if one group is superior, aren't the others necessarily *in*ferior?

My research work on "Immigration and Acculturation" showed ways in which Asian Indians are driven to live out 'superior' minority myths and stereotypes before one another and before the general public. Living a façade of success renders Asian Indian immigrants reluctant to seek therapy whatever the stress, even when most desperately needed, because of the fear of stigmatizing not only the person who needs help but also that person's entire extended family.

The cultural proscription of Asian Indians prohibits them from talking about personal, intimate problems with anyone other than a member of the family; and so therapeutic help is shunned, even when the results prove disastrous.

Reena was an iconic example. She approached therapy with immense hesitation and uncertainty. Every few steps forward involved nearly as many steps back. It took several email exchanges and an initial introductory telephone session before she felt even remotely 'comfortable' enough to come and see me in person.

But those emails were compelling. She sent me a lengthy description of herself, a near-flowchart of her family dynamics, a list of the current issues that she would like to explore in our conversations. Her organized approach to therapy impressed me greatly. From her emails, Reena certainly did not seem a 'mess.' Her comments had the clarity, energy and discipline that was the very picture of member of a 'model minority.'

But the reality was very, very far from the presentation.

The Reena that arrived in my office that first time seemed a complete mess. She was in her thirties, unkempt, with long hair and baggy sweats that both needed a wash. She dragged her feet to my office with obvious reluctance, looking around nervously, anxious and jittery throughout the entire session.

"Reena," I said, trying to make her relax and feel comfortable, "I know it's not easy for everyone to walk in a therapist's office. I know it takes courage sometimes, and I appreciate that you're brave to have taken that first step. But this isn't an interrogation. I'm not here to judge you or condemn you. This is a place where you can say whatever you want, *be* whoever you *are*, without judgment or condemnation ever entering the picture."

"I wish I had done this years ago," she mumbled. "I *so* needed to talk to someone then. There was so much going on inside me. I was exploding! But my parents never believed in therapy. And they're supposed to be *'Doctors'*," she said, snarling the word.

Almost at once her anger deflated back to a blank depression.

"But I *am* to blame for my condition, aren't I?" she said. "Who else is to blame for what I am if not me? I disappoint everyone. Everyone. Even my-self."

"There are eight billion people in the world, Reena. You can't have disappointed every last one. Who exactly did you disappoint'?

"My parents, my family, my aunts and uncles and cousins. My ancestors. My culture. My herit-age. My 'caste.' All of India! 'Model minority'?" She laughed bitterly. "I'm *disgusting.*"

She spoke while trying not to cry. I could feel the lump in her throat, the tightness in her chest.

"I am *such a disgrace.* After all that my parents did for me. They've done *so much.* And here, here I am, a complete failure. I *hate* myself."

She reached for the tissue box.

I was intentionally quiet, giving her a moment to gather her emotions.

She looked up at me. "You're originally from India, Doctor Pandey."

"I was born in India. Raised among Indians, yes."

"Then you know what it's like in our culture. There's *no* second place, *no* awards for effort. You're supposed to be the *best.* If you're not the *best*, you're *garbage*, you're *nothing.*" She wiped her eyes. "I'm sure your parents gave you the same speech too."

I nodded. But added, "My parents did want me to be the best—at whatever I wanted to be. But I wanted that too. We were in agreement, so there wasn't any problem. Were things different bet-ween you and your parents?"

She almost screamed. "Yes! *Yes!* Things were *totally* different!" Again the intensity of her self-assertion collapsed almost as quickly as it burst out.

"But they were right. Always right about everything. They sacrificed for me. They gave me a wonderful life full of luxury and comfort. And I've crushed their dreams. I'm a *disgrace!*"

It was painful to watch her, and hard to maintain my proper objectivity. The self-loathing she exhibited. The wretchedness. The sadness. I empathized with her deeply, and yet I fully understood the 'model minority' mindset of her parents. I shared many of her cultural beliefs, and many of the beliefs of her parents, too. I was quite familiar with the immigrant generation, and their drive to spur, to *force* their children to be 'successfully launched" in the world.

But there are different varieties of success, and one generation's definition is not always that of the next.

As Reena went on, however, I was puzzled as to exactly what the nature of her great failure was, and also why she was reacting the way she did.

After all, the woman in front of me was an adult. A highly successful adult! She might dress and act more like an unkempt young teenager with parental issues. Nonetheless the woman in front of me was an attractive, highly paid, licensed corporate attorney. A graduate of Duke University and Harvard Law School. A prominent figure in a major

Chicago law firm that specialized in high-level corporate takeovers. What sort of 'failure' exactly was she talking about?

Before me was a serious achiever—and yet a high achiever, she told me, currently on leave from her firm after being hospitalized as an inpatient for severe panic attack and chest pain. A high achiever—and an alcoholic. A high-functioning alcoholic, to be sure.

Reena explained to me that both her parents were physicians who moved to the United States for their residency after finishing medical school in India. They lived in a wealthy neighborhood in Portland, Oregon, where her father worked as a resident surgeon, while her mother worked at another hospital as chief cardiologist. Their schedules were massively overbooked, and Reena and her younger brother Nitin were brought up by a series of polished servants and English-accented governesses.

Nitin was born when Reena started kindergarten, but the siblings' childhood was not like most American childhoods. Her immigrant parents were obsessive about hard work, striving for success, financial security. They were determined to set their children onto the 'right' career paths from the very start. The strings of governesses were accompanied by strings of accomplished tutors from as early as Reena could remember.

She did not remember as much about her childhood experience with her parents. They were too rarely there. They were not completely without affection or generosity. They bought her gifts and took her and Nitin on wonderful vacations. But work took first place, child-raising second, and every appearance included a rigid one- and two-word lecture: Study. Study hard. Study! Study hard!

A certain aloofness was passed along to Reena. She made no friends in elementary and middle school—she was too busy being whisked away by tutors and governesses for extra-curricular studies and activities.

She grew up with high expectations, the highest possible expectations. Exemplary performance at her academic subjects was expected. No, *demanded.*

And not just academic excellence. As early as elementary school, she was also enrolled in swimming classes, classical Indian dance classes, tennis, golf.

Was she especially interested in swimming, classical Indian dance, tennis or golf? The question was never asked, not even by Reena.

Reena continued all these activities, along with her studies, throughout elementary school and high school. The competition was tough and top grades and excellence were expected, in classrooms and in sports and activities. In everything: in appearance, in dress, in speech, in posture.

Home was not an issue: Reena never had to worry about chores and domestic responsibilities. Hired help was available for that. Her mother bragged about her lack of domestic skills.

"Poor Reena! She doesn't even know how to boil water!"

As for her father, time and again he would recite his mantra: "All you have to do is be the best. Always. At everything." He would say it again and again, throughout her childhood and adolescence. "Be the best, the *best*, better than anyone else.

"Be the best and you will rule the world."

But as Reena grew, it dawned on her that she didn't want to rule the world. What she wanted was to be an artist. She was talented, extremely talented, and she loved expressing herself through drawing and painting. At her seventh-grade school art exhibit, she won the first prize for her work.

But being the best at art was not the kind of excellence favored by her parents. It was an excellence her parents ridiculed.

"Reena. Do you know what artists *make?* Nothing! Do you know what they are? They're degenerates! Is that your plan, to be a starving artist? Are you going to live in our basement for the rest of your life?"

No one encouraged Reena to explore what she would have preferred to explore, or asked her what she wanted to do or what appealed to her. Instead, to hear Reena tell it, they relentlessly promoted and defended and imposed *their* choice of classes and *their* choice of activities.

And if the workload was overwhelming and the stress exceptional, they defended that too.

"All this is for *you,* Reena, we want the best for *you.* Other parents just don't care as much about their children's future as we do. We're doing all this because we *love* you, Reena."

What could she say? She had no say. The pressure to give in and please her parents was constant, non-stop. Eventually, unsurprisingly, she gave in, as did her brother.

Parents set the agenda. Children complied. That was the way of things in the Indian community. End of story.

What was their agenda for Reena? A medical career. She was to follow in the footsteps of her parents. She had no interest whatever in biology and science, but that didn't matter. She was "forced," she said, to take Advanced Placement courses in biology and anatomy in high school.

Her parents ordained that Reena would excel at those subjects, then get into medical school, get her degree, and become a medical practitioner. Like them.

With her parents' ample resources and professional reach, they even secured an internship for her during her senior year in high school.

"An internship," I said. "That's impressive."

"I *hated* it."

But Reena's resentment was smothered by an even more intense emotion: guilt. As she matured into her late teens, she concealed her growing anger and rage under the pressure of that shame. Her parents were doing so much for her, they gave her so much. She lived in splendor, in luxury. She *owed* them. She *should* make them happy, *should* fulfill their lofty expectations.

What did they want from her, what did they need to make her happy? Only for Reena to excel in a high-status power profession to their liking.

That would make them happy. Was that so much? Wasn't giving them only fair, after all they had given her?

She tried. She tried very hard. Reena did go on to excel at those things her parents wanted Reena to excel at. She excelled at golf enough to secure a scholarship at Duke, where she was told to select pre-med classes. That she did.

Her parents were delighted, and saw to it that her luxurious lifestyle followed her throughout her college days as well. They arranged for a luxury apartment off-campus for her during her studies, a cleaning service for her, a chauffeur service for her.

They spared no expense. Reena would give her full attention to her studies, and thus scale the heights, just as her parents did.

Only it didn't quite work out that way.

The affluence, the excess, was seductive; and Reena gave in to it. But far from direct parental oversight, she found a new sense of freedom in college. She started enjoying her wealthy reputation and her 'model minority' status. She joined the top sorority, and became the 'it' girl.

It was inevitable. She was tall, young, beautiful, with a willowy height of five foot ten and a petite weight of 115 pounds. She looked like a model. On occasion she *did* model for fashion magazines, whose recruiters wandered college campuses looking for new talent. She was a campus notable, a star—a cool rich kid surrounded by wannabes. Where other students had to work hard to support their college education, and struggled and scraped to keep their scholarship, Reena lived in extravagance and self-indulgence.

"Life was a party," said Reena, wistfully. "A party that never stopped."

"After all the pressure you were under in high school, it must have felt pretty liberating."

"It did," she said, "until it stopped."

"What happened?"

"What do you think?" she snapped. But then she added, quietly, "I'm sorry... I'm sorry, Doctor Pandey, but what do I think happened? Suddenly I was popular. People wanted to be around me. I was invited to parties. There were drinks. There were drugs. There were boys. I *liked* being the center of attention, I *liked* going to parties, I liked getting stoned and going out and dancing all night; and I hated, I just *hated* going to med classes. So, I, well, I just... stopped going."

"You dropped out?"

"I wasn't sober enough to drop out. Everything became a haze. I skipped classes, I stopped reading the textbooks, I stopped turning my papers in on time. I knew what would eventually happen, but—I just *hated medicine*. I hated blood and bodies and all that—*yucky* stuff. I could not *stand* the subject. So, I went to parties to get away from it.

"I ended up being drunk half the time, stoned the other half. Things got bad, then got worse. I began missing assignments, throwing away letters of warning. On top of the drinking, I started binge-eating, then purging, then sleeping all day to recover."

She shrugged.

"I just fell apart."

"There must have been repercussions," I said.

"*Oh*, yes," she said. "There were repercussions. I lost my scholarship. My sorority kicked me out in my sophomore year. My grades? They crashed through the floor. It was so bad they put me on academic probation. I couldn't deal with it. I retreated into alcohol and marijuana. That became my reality. My *only* reality. I'd lock myself in my room for days and just drink and... hide."

"What about your parents?"

"I kept in touch with them regularly. Or maybe I should say that I lied to them regularly. I called them, sent them letters, and lied, lied, lied. I duped them into believing that I was doing fine."

"When did they catch on?"

"When they got a letter from the Dean about my GPA dropping below 2.0, and about my being put on probation. I knew they'd find out sooner or later. I thought that when they did, their heads would explode!"

"Did their heads explode?"

She shook her head. "No. I was shocked. And... thankful. Grateful. So grateful. I felt so... ashamed, so guilty."

"They weren't angry?"

"Oh, they were *angry*. I could see that. But they were afraid, too. Afraid for me. I think it was because when they confronted me, I just went completely to pieces. It all spilled out. They didn't have to beat me up—I beat myself up good. They were shocked. I think they were afraid I'd run away completely or kill myself of something. I don't know what it was, but when they saw what a complete mess I'd become, they took me out of Duke right on the spot and brought me home.

"I was depressed and disgusted and disappointed with myself, and they didn't blame me at all. Well, they didn't blame me outright. They wanted me to recover, and they were physicians, so they treated me as though I was in recovery. They arranged private care and put me through a kind of detox. They talked to Duke and arranged a sabbatical. Officially I had gone home for a semester break. Then they sent me away to India, to live with my grandparents for six months, to work on myself there, and get back on track."

"It sounds as though they love you very much."

"I know they do. That's what makes what I did to them so terrible."

"What happened? Did you get back on track?"

"On *their* track. After a six-month break, we had a big family meeting. My father and mother proposed a compromise. I could choose any major I liked. *But* I had to remain at Duke. That was nonnegotiable. 'Richard Nixon went to Duke, said Mom. 'It's produced five Nobel Laureates and fifty Rhodes Scholars,' said Dad. I couldn't care less, but I didn't say a word. Dad did, and it was the last word: Duke lent prestige not only to me but to the entire family. The whole family, the entire clan, would be *impressed* if I graduated from Duke. They could brag about me to their friends and associates, if I stayed at Duke.

"But not if I washed out. So, staying was mandatory. A break was fine. Even a stretch of bad grades was not the end of the world. but for their daughter to be a *drop-out?* That was unthinkable. Unacceptable. The impression they worked to spread in their upper-echelon circle was that 'Reena needed a year off from college to explore India'! What a sham!

"So, you went to India. But then you went back to Duke."

Reena nodded. "I didn't want to go back. But I went back."

Things were somewhat different now for Reena at Duke. She stayed, but she was allowed to major in art and fashion design, subjects she like and cared about. She gave them the attention and interest she had never given medicine. So, in time, she graduated with honors.

But the family crisis was not over. Nor was Reena's personal crisis.

Prescription drugs are abundant in physician families, and as part of her recovery, her parents put her on anti-depressants and stimulants. Drugs would give her a better academic focus and improve her concentration. If that's what it took, it was a price worth paying, and they made Reena pay it whether she wanted to or not.

She was shocked. Throughout high school she always took pride in doing everything by her own merit. She had 'model minority' immigrant pride, and strove always to be better than her native-born Americans.

Now her performance and focus had plunged below the level of mediocrity, and if medication was needed to the meet that mark, her parents insisted on it. They had strongly condemned her for using drugs—then put her on a wide range of other drugs of which *they* approved.

Again, agency had been stripped away from her, as well as her own self-respect.

Her parents paid less and less attention to Reena's emotional struggles. As they had said since her very childhood, studies and grades were all that mattered.

And this time around they took a direct hand. They appeared on her college campus on a regular basis now to make sure she was on track with her classes. Her mother even got reports from the food delivery and cleaning and other services she'd arranged for Reena, "so that Reena won't have to worry about such minor hassles," an arrangement that left Reena feeling untrusted and spied upon.

Reena continued to stay in the sort of lavish campus apartment to which her parents had accustomed her. But alone. No more parties, no sororities, no visitors. Nor did Reena socialize with others. Her parents made it clear that she needed to make up for lost time. She all but imprisoned herself in the college library.

The strict oversight worked: She did, after all, graduate with honors, though only with a 'lowly' art and fashion design degree. Her parents were relieved. Reena was gratified too: a measure of her self-respect had been restored.

But then another non-negotiable parental demand was issued. A degree in art and fashion had been acceptable, barely, as a preliminary step to a higher academic institution. But a *career* in art and fashion? No. Her parents gave her a flat command: she was to apply immediately for Harvard Law.

Reena protested. Her dream was to pursue a higher degree on her own in fashion design at a re-nowned institute in Rome. Once again, her dreams came crashing down as her parents took charge of her life. She was told, over and over, that among people of her parent's class and among the high-charged Indian-American community to which they belonged, a degree in art was an embarrass-ment. The only careers that *really* counted were the careers of high-paying professional in medi-cine and law. *Other* children of immigrants knew that. *Other* such model minority children were aiming for the stars, they said. Reena was aiming for the gutter, where forgotten starving artists went to die.

It was not negotiable. Reena would go to Har-vard and study Law. Period.

She complied. As always.

Reena took the LSAT and passed with flying colors. Her parents were delighted. As a gift, she was given an all-expense paid summer trip to Paris before joining Harvard Law School. It was a wild, wonderful, glorious summer, she said—her last, because after that, several numbing years followed of laboring for a law degree she did not want, so as to practice a profession she could not stand, in or-der to get a high-status-position at corporate law office which she loathed.

Reena's parents were happy. Reena herself? She spent most evenings quietly drinking herself into oblivion.

Americans—insular Americans, ones born here with little to no familiarity with India or Indian-American culture—have rather outdated ideas about the Indian-American community. They still think of India as an affair of turbans, gurus, and Gunga Din. There may know of a few Indian computer programmers here and there, but for the most part India remains (in their minds) a land of poverty, esoteric spirituality and fasting fakirs.

The spiritual and mystical resources of historic India are quite real; in fact, genuinely profound. But they have nothing whatever to do with the hard new materialism of the existing Indian-American upper class community. In today's upper-class Indian communities, status and success, monetary and professional eminence—*pre*-eminence—have become everything. Reena's parents belonged utterly to that country club culture and its lavish Indian-American lifestyle. They were a 'poster couple' who had *made it* in the wealthiest country in the world. They glittered and shone, and they wanted their bright light to be blinding.

Regrettably, it was: it blinded them to a painful darkness behind their wealthy façade.

Reena's father Roy was a fine physician. But also a man of deeply compromised morals—a womanizer and an adulterer. He would go on sex escapades with women half his age. He had mistresses in different cities, and lavished money on them. He would pay for their luxury condos, buy them expensive cars, jewelry, dresses. Twice every year he would go to Vegas for a 'boys' trip' with his colleagues, where gambling, drugs and strip clubs was all he cared for.

Her mother knew, had always known, and was livid. Reena knew too. She was all too aware of her parents' fights after their drunken weekend parties. They broke things, smashed furniture, even attacked each other physically. It was the norm. At times she was afraid enough of their screams and rage to hide and sleep in the servant's quarters.

The glittering façade they presented hid all of that. To the world they were the 'perfect couple,' the model minority. They were famous in their circles for arriving at others' parties in their chauffeur-driven Bentley, and drowning those invited to their own parties with rivers of the rarest and most expensive of wines.

Reena's mother might be aware of her husband's extramarital affairs and debauchery. But she too was addicted to the luxurious lifestyle of a 'perfect couple.'

As for practicing medicine? Professionally, so far as Reena knew, they were both completely competent and highly respected. But for neither parent was medicine a true calling, in Reena's view. Just one more status symbol among many.

After a few sessions, Reena confessed to me that she wasn't ashamed only of her own self-condemned ingratitude, or her academic struggles or her drinking. She was ashamed of her parents too—her father's adulteries, her mother's hurt acceptance of it, their flamboyant but fundamentally hypocritical lifestyle. I saw that Reena's shame had many levels, and a good deal of nuance—a life of emotional secrecy, which she was slowly beginning to reveal to me.

Then one day she confessed a major secret. Reena was involved with a man. A man twice her age. And a Caucasian.

His name was Carter, and he was divorced with two grown-up children. 'Children' nearly as old as Reena. She didn't care. She loved him, she said. They'd been living together for over four years, and they were planning to get married, she said.

However, neither seemed in any great hurry to do so.

I could think of two reasons why.

"Do your parents know about this relationship?"

"Are you *joking?* They would *kill* me! Carter's almost as old as my father! He's not an Indian. He's not a Hindu. He's not even *rich*—he's an art professor at a local college. It's not even Ivy League! There's no way they'd ever agree to our getting married. They'd send me back to India again!"

"Do you love this man?"

"I guess..."

"So what do you intend to do about the situation?"

She shrugged.

"Drink myself silly," she said.

That wasn't a solution, and we both knew it. I didn't have to pressure her by saying it. I didn't want Reena to feel that she was disappointing me too, and to add me to the list of all those people she felt she was letting down.

"Reena, listen," I said. "Love is a gift. It isn't a transaction. It's freely, generously given. Your parents aren't perfect either, but you still love them, don't you, even so? They aren't going to stop caring about you either, even if you make some personal choices they don't like. You don't have to pretend you're something you're not just because you think it will make others happy. You don't have to live up to an idea of perfection that isn't yours.

"Yes, you owe your parents gratitude and respect and thanks. But not mindless obedience. And certainly not self-destructive obedience. What you do owe them is your honesty. And the way to start this is by being honest with yourself first. Is the life you're living now the life you want to live? If not, you need to re-examine yourself and your life, and begin to make some changes. Changes that will help make your life into what *you* want it to be."

Reena nodded. But didn't commit to making any changes, and didn't return for the next session. In fact, she stayed away for several weeks.

I suspected—correctly, as it turned out—that she'd be back. She was caught up in self-destructive patterns in behavior that brought intermittent moments of collapse and chaos into her life, and left her suffering chronic self-abuse and self-debasement in her thoughts. As long as the negative thoughts and behaviors persisted, the negative results would persist.

Sure enough: she didn't want to talk about the man she was seeing, or face the situation, and so she began to skip sessions again. Thanks to these emotional ups and downs, her work began to suffer. Once again, she turned to alcohol to numb the difficult feelings. Once again it didn't work. Soon she was having panic and anxiety symptoms again.

One day I received the expected call: Reena had been admitted to a local trauma center for severe chest pain after passing out at the office.

We began meeting regularly again.

I confess: I was happy to see her back in my office. Even after just a few short sessions, she had come to mean a great deal to me.

Now at this point in Reena's story, some readers may protest.

"My God, Rashmi, there are people who would *kill* for a chance to go to Harvard Law School. This woman you're treating is rich, beautiful! She models for magazines! A college Professor wants to marry her. She's a corporate attorney making God knows how much money. She has parents providing her cooks, chauffeurs, an all-expense-paid summer in Paris! You call this *suffering?* You *sympathize?* You're just taking her side—presenting this spoiled, shallow, pampered creature as some sort of victim, and her hard-working loving parents as villains."

Not at all. What I want to do in this book is show readers the reality of therapy—"what it's like, how it works."

And the reality is that, as my client, Reena taught me things about therapy as a profession, and even about myself, that I had not suspected. In that regard, Reena's treatment was a revelation. I learned that therapy can be as much a journey of self-understanding for the therapist as it is for the client.

Yes. I *did* sympathize with Reena. Why not? We came from not dissimilar backgrounds. I too knew the constant pressure to excel that comes with being a member of the 'model minority.' Pressure not just from parents, but from peers, acquaintances, more distant relatives, the entire immigrant community.

I was luckier than Reena: I had two wonderful parents prepared to support me whatever my career choice. But whatever that choice was, they still expected excellence of me.

It wasn't out of sadism. Expecting excellence from others, from oneself, was a cultural given, it was in the air we breathed. I wanted excellence for myself too.

But I *understood* how Reena could feel crushed by it, I had *felt* that pressure myself, just as I now felt *guilt* for having so much more open and tolerant a set of parents than poor Reena.

I had stumbled upon something I did not expect to be a part of therapy: a kind of *attunement*: an empathic relatedness, a not-quite-oneness wherein feelings are shared by client and therapist. It was not a matter of my being a therapist indifferently observing a client from a distant outside perspective. I was *like* her. I could stand in her shoes. There was a resonance.

I found myself taking her side. But also catching myself, reminding myself that I was not there primarily to sympathize, but to heal. We were on the same wavelength, but remained two distinct voices.

I had not expected therapy to be so much of a personal encounter. After all, in a hospital setting, there is always a certain institutional distance. A clinical psychologist and a patient are never even alone together, never one-on-one. There are always other practitioners nearby, residents, interns, nurses, security guards to call if things get out of hand. There are always tasks to do, paperwork to fill out. One looks in, makes notes, and moves on. A professional tone is maintained.

But a therapist's office is not that. A therapy session is not less the analysis of the professional than a drama of the confessional. It is a long-term relationship sometimes marked by searing, heartbreaking emotional episodes. It can involve cool analysis, and often does, and must; but just as often, one becomes emotionally involved, one is *moved*; deeply involved, deeply moved. Not so deeply that the professional relationship of therapist to client is erased, but deeply enough to gain the client's trust, hope and confidence.

And deeply enough to learn, as well as heal. Some readers may view a client like Reena as pampered and privileged. I can assure you that few clients in the course of my career ever displayed so much sheer naked *pain* as Reena. No client ever showed me more forcefully the awesome power of thoughts alone to torment and cripple—and to restore—the self.

There is nothing novel about that observation. From Buddha to the Roman Stoics to Aaron Beck, sages have told us that it is not the things that happen to us that cause us pain, but rather the way we *interpret* those things. Parental advice can be taken kind and loving—or dictatorial and coercive. A trip to Paris can be a gift—or a bribe. Gratitude can be uplifting, if free and spontaneous; or a crushing burden, if demanded and mandatory.

No one made me more aware of the power of awareness, of frameworks of interpretation, of thoughts, than Reena. Reena did in fact have a wonderfully rich life, excellent personal qualities, hundreds of things to cherish and celebrate. Yet somehow, she managed to transmute all that into *agony*, a pure agony so intense that only alcoholic stupor could make it go away.

That 'somehow' is a misuse of language, however. It's very clear why Reena was so wretched: she constantly *told* herself she was wretched; that her entire life was wretched; that her past and future were wretched. She would wallow in fits of misery telling herself that her parents controlled her life completely, that she had no freedom, and that she was guilty in some unforgivable cosmic way for not being happy about it.

"Reena," I would say, "your parents don't control your life. *You* do. You're financially independent. As free as a bird. You could walk out that door and start a completely new life anywhere in the world. If you don't like the way your life has turned out, why not just do something else? And if your parents don't like it—so what? You've had to live with their life choices. Maybe it's time they learned to live with yours."

Heresy! Blasphemy! Reena would literally cover her ears not to hear.

Eventually, though, the words got through—not because they were directives ordering her to change, but because they were questions, questions asking her to examine her true feelings, her own beliefs. They were part of a long conversation aimed at trying to get Reena to look at her life and her problems in a new, fresh, more effective way—a way likely to lead to more happiness and personal fulfillment.

Working with Reena convinced me of the sheer power of the words in our heads, the power of the things we say to ourselves. It also showed me the value and effectiveness of thoughtfully—*mindfully,* as we say today—examining those words, taking a close critical look at the things we say to ourselves.

Should one really feel *guilty* for not wanting to be a doctor or a lawyer? Some people are just not attracted to those jobs. What's wrong with that?

We may love our parents, but does that make them good career counselors? It's certainly reasonable to consult one's parents and to seek their advice. But it's even more reasonable to consult oneself, to consult one's own preferences and inclinations—to know oneself.

I knew this intellectually. But it was quite another thing to see these negative internal monologues play out at length in a living person—in a client in one's charge.

In my hospital work prior to opening a private clinical practice, things were different. The people a clinical psychologist deals with in a hospital setting are quite definitely not rich, successful, or coming from parties in Paris on their way to Harvard Law School. Treatment, regrettably, is focused more on sedating them with prescription drugs rather weaning them off the recreational drugs they swallow by engaging them in Socratic dialogue. Time is limited, and work schedules pass you along from one person to the next. Compassion is there, but a compassion of the surface, quick, cool and impersonal.

With Reena, however, I began to see the depth and power of unexamined ideas, assumptions, and beliefs. She showed me the extraordinary force of internal dialogue. Her life was misery incarnate, yet why? She was young, wealthy, dazzlingly attractive, intelligent, talented, well-educated, embarked on a career track most anyone would envy. But her descriptions of inner life were the stuff of nightmare.

As I learned to better understand the primacy of interpretations, the harrowing impact of such unexamined internal dialogue, I could see Reena's adversity in more depth—as well as a way out.

Reena was literally in agony, but what drove her was not the objective facts making up her life, but her perspective on them. She was expert at self-condemnation, but devoid of self-examination. Her inner monologue was a litany of continual self-abuse: she *had* to be perfect, *had* to obey her parents, *had* to hide her romantic relationship, *had* to labor away at classes and careers she could not stand.

Why did she *have* to do these things? Because she *told* herself, over and over, every day, that she had to.

Why did she feel so miserable all the time? Because if she wasn't happy about doing the things she *had* to do, then she was a *bad person*, a *monster*, an *embarrassment,* a *disgrace.*

Was any of this true? Or, like the elements of a bad dream, did all of it simply fade away when looked at soberly, in the waking light of day?

I helped Reena look at these beliefs and statements and assumptions in that light. Were the things she was saying to herself true? Did they make sense? Was there another way she could frame things, understand things? Could she imagine other ways of looking at things, handling things?

I posed the questions, and Reena's mindful consideration chipped away at the blockages. Gradually they loosened their grip.

But Reena changed me too. She was, after all, my first Indian-American client. I very much wanted my treatment to be successful. But how to best approach her? Should I present as an emotionally even, all-accepting, Carl Rogers brand of passive sounding-wall? Should I argue her out of her self-lacerating ideas with passionate logic (and a certain amount of swearing), like Albert Ellis? Should I gaze at her dispassionately, like Mr. Spock, or be her friend and confidante, like Dr. Ruth?

Therapists develop their own 'style' as time goes on, but I was still green, still learning as I went along.

And I realized too that behind the figure of Reena stood the ghost of Martha. Was Reena so unhappy that she too might take her own life? No? Could I be sure?

I learned that I had to put away the fiction of being at a distance. I came to see that our relationship—every serious relationship of therapist to client—is a personal encounter. I learned I needed to be mindful too: to acknowledge that I approached my relationship with this client, with every client, with thoughts and beliefs of my own. I had to be mindful of my own thoughts and assumptions, and examine not just the client but myself as the conversation proceeds.

This is why I speak of *attunement*. I was not sitting at a distance, looking at Reena from the outside. Nor was I merely sympathizing, or expressing empathy. Strangely, gradually—and therapeutically—we were harmonizing.

After all, why wouldn't we? Between us we shared India, the Indian-American community, Indian-American culture. I knew it so well, and loved and hated it with equal measure. I knew the massive ambition, the parochial attitudes, the demand to excel, and the guilt over 'letting the community down' if one displayed anything less than meticulous perfection.

Because I could see that, and see it from Reena's perspective, I could help her step away—if that was her wish. I could *help* her step away, but I couldn't and wouldn't pull or drag her away. Her parents had tried that, with disastrous results.

A therapist helps the client find *their* way. We foster self-examination: we don't shape the choices that self-examination poses, or the direction in which it leads.

Reena told me that she'd felt disconnected and depressed for a very long time. Her family and friends never supplied appropriate support, nor did they encourage her to share her feelings. But how could they ever know her feelings if she never shared them? She'd suppressed her feelings, her emotional struggles, her drinking, her eating disorder as early as high school. She'd kept it up more or less effectively throughout college—well, except for being put on probation and getting caught lying about it, and going completely to bits in front of her parents when confronted.

It was not a great strategy, but most of the time it was a strategy that got her through the day, and she had gotten used to living that way and seeing things that way. Wear a mask till you fall apart, and afterwards put the mask back on. It looked as though she intended to stay with that strategy through grad school and into her professional career and beyond.

I felt for Reena. If my father and mother had not been as tolerant and supportive, who knows… but I was learning to follow my own cognitive-behavioral advice: I noticed and acknowledged my responses, and tried to use them for more rational ends. My own slight feeling of guilt helped me to understand hers.

In some ways Reena was as much a help to me professionally as I was to her therapeutically. She got me off on the right foot, as it were, as a newly practicing therapist. Working with Reena was *not* like working with Martha, with oversight from overworked and distant authorities, mandatory medication, rules and limitations. There were guidelines in private practice, yes, but there was also time, focus, a space for empathy, a capacity for connection, for self-reflection on my part as well as the clients.

Reena showed me things about therapy that I had never expected to see—that therapy could be *funny*. Even hilarious.

Consider an example:

The topic of introducing Carter to her parents was the elephant in the room. Always there, always avoided. In our therapy hour each week, I would raise the subject, and she would carefully and pointedly change the subject each time.

Finally, one day I brought it out directly.

"Reena. When are you going to introduce Carter to your parents? You say you want to get married. You can't get married and hide it from them. You understand that, yes?"

"I'm not ready... why *hurry* things?... I'm doing OK... Carter's good with it... they're happy... there's peace in my life... sort of... should I really push things? ... I don't know..."

"Why keep putting it off? You live with him. You say you intend to marry him. It has to come out sometime. This is about who you are, Reena. How you deal with things. You can't keep running away forever. You need to face things, not avoid them."

"No matter how understanding *you* are, Rashmi, the Indian community isn't. They still look down upon marrying outside the community. As for my dad, he's *extremely* conservative when it comes to marriage. I told my brother about Carter and I, and even he's against it. Dad is in his Seventies... he has a heart condition... I don't want to cause him stress... What if something happens?"

She started crying.

"We both know how widespread patriarchal control is in the Indian community, Reena," I said. "But what is your option? You're approaching thirty-five. You say you want to get married and be a mother. The biological clock ticking away, and we've talked about your anxiety in that regard. What does putting things off do to your chances of having children? It's not going to get any better the longer you wait. Besides—you love Carter! Right?"

"I do, Dr. Pandey... it's just... this will be the first time anyone in the family—anyone in the whole community has married an outsider! I grew up hearing, 'Sure, it's okay to *date* these people, but when you *marry*, you have to marry within your own community.' You know how it is. All my cousins, even my brother, have dated outsiders. But when he got married, he married the Indian girl he dated in med school!"

I confess to feeling a spark of anger. Consorting with outsiders wasn't a crime large enough to prevent her father from what Reena described as a lifetime of adulterous encounters with outsiders. But it was bad enough to keep his daughter from marrying the man she loved?

I held myself in check The question was not what I thought of marrying outside the community, or even what her parents thought about it, but what Reena thought about it. Or rather, why Reena was afraid even to think about it.

"I'd still encourage you to speak with your parents and introduce Carter. Putting things off only reinforces the behavior of putting things off. Nothing changes, and a situation that causes you pain and anxiety only persists. Besides, do you ever think about how this feels from Carter's perspective? He's living in the dark about the future of this relationship. What about *his* feelings? Maybe he thinks you're ashamed of him. You care about the parents you love, but what about the man you love?"

She sat there in silence for a while. "But... but what will people *say?*"

I smiled without saying anything.

I expected a long wait. To my great surprise, Reena emailed me the next day. She'd called her parents and told them about Carter.
They immediately wanted to meet him.
They arranged to meet that very weekend.
    They did.
It was a *disaster!*

Her mom cried her heart out once Carter left, said Reena. She begged break off the relationship. He was *too old!* He was old enough to be her *father!* Her *Grandfather!* Old enough to be *dead!* He had *grown-up children!* He was (ugh) an *art* professor! He was an *American!* He was *white!* He was *Christian!* He was, he was—she could barely say the word—he was *poor!*

I hesitate to share with readers what Reena's father said.

I'll share what her father did: He insisted on having an emergency session right away. With everyone. Reena. Carter. Himself. Myself. Her mother. Her mom's sister. Her mom's sister's husband. Uncles. Aunts. Cousins. Second cousins. Friends of the family. Half of the clan was planning to attend!

I had to book an entire conference room!
Prime Minister Modi would officiate!
Yes, all right: I exaggerate. But not by much.
The beauty of personal therapy is its privacy, its intimacy. This was beyond even group therapy. This was Super Bowl therapy!

But, as I knew all too well, it was also how such 'model minorities' operated.

I steeled myself, and penciled the date in.

The group meeting was... interesting. Reena's father, the stately patriarch, walked slowly in his dark suit and dark hat. He had a cane. His wife, head bent, in somewhat traditional garb, face in mourning, accompanied him.

They sat at the center of a long large corporate oval table in silence. Uncle and Aunt joined in a bit later. Slowly the crowd accumulated around them. Reena, Carter and I were at the opposite end, isolated and leprous.

The father, though shorter than I, looked down at me from across the table from great Olympian heights, sizing me up, and dismissing me with a look of utterly nauseated contempt.

I could read the non-verbal commentary in his cold lofty expression.

"You... you *therapist*," his expression seemed to sneer, "what do *you* know about our family, our complications, our pride, our eminence, our sufferings... you were probably born yesterday, you irksome little girl... you child... you *intern!*"

I looked back cool as a cucumber.

I greeted them all politely, and initiated the session with Reena's relationship dilemma. Though, really, it was not a dilemma at all, I said. Marriage is a relationship between a man and a woman. This man and this woman loved each other, and wished to marry. They had every legal right to do so, and no need to ask for permission from the family. They *wanted* the family's blessing, true. And if the family genuinely loved Reena, then, generously, they would give it. So, Reena and Carter hoped.

But they had no power whatever to coerce Reena or Carter. The decision was theirs. They could support that decision, or cause the couple and themselves continuing pain and suffering by opposing it. Would they make things painful for everyone concerned, or give their blessing? It was up to them.

The dad cleared his throat.

"As you know... being an Indian yourself... *'Doctor'* Pandey... we are the keepers of our culture and tradition," he began. "A long, great, noble culture and tradition. A way of life our people have cherished and preserved for thousands—thousands!—of years. We are *in* this country now, but we are not *of* it. We are our culture and our ways, and we need to preserve those ways, to teach and pass on those ways to our next generation, to maintain the *uniqueness* of our *priceless culture*, or we will lose everything, and become like... well... *Americans.*"

He said the word as though it were some food item in his throat rising up and making him gag.

Turning his head, he looked with a shudder of disgust at Carter, as he imagined rap-drunk American grandchildren eating monster cheeseburgers.

"What will happen to *us* if we begin marrying (ugh) *Christians* and (ugh) *Jews*. What will become of us if we betray our ancestors, our parents' parents' parents, and dissolve into a shapeless faceless mass? Where will our very identity go?"

I realized I was in, not for a reasonable discussion, but for a major seminar lecture.

He went on (and on), reciting own life story, his long family history, his passionate concerns about the sacred need to preserve holy Indian culture, to preserve the moral and ethical ideal of being the very model of a model minority, about helping hundreds of other Indians migrate and getting them jobs, about opening schools and hospitals in India for the poor, about sacred Hindu principles and sacrosanct Brahminic traditions. The list was as never ending as his grandiose sense of self.

It was hard to reconcile his majestic oratory with images of him regularly partying with the boys amid assorted multicultural hookers in private rooms at Las Vegas casinos.

That said, his presentation provided insight. I could see what Reena must have gone through. No wonder she was so scared, so mentally beaten up. He wasn't simply a manipulative father. He brought the whole weight of Indian civilization down on her head like a hammer.

I avoided that trap by simply brushing it aside. As he went on about Krishna and Arjuna, I interrupted and went straight to issue.

"Sir," I said. "Reena loves Carter and *intends* to marry him. She would *like* your support and acceptance. She doesn't *need* it. She and Carter can marry if that's what they want to do. You can't stop them, but you *can* add pain and misery to Reena's life by your words and attitudes opposing them. Why bother? Why not simply let her marry whom she wants, accept her personal choices for herself, and wish her well?"

"That's *utter nonsense!*" the little man thundered. "She needs to marry an accomplished surgeon! I know the very man Reena needs. In fact, we've known each other for years! He's the son of one of my oldest friends. The only son. He's going to inherit a *fortune!* He's *perfect!*"

"And anyway, who's going to marry Reena at *her* age?" peeped Reena's mother, at her husband's elbow. "We're lucky we got father's choice to agree to his proposal at all. But if he hears about *this*," she said, sneaking a look of horror at Carter.

Further comment was superfluous.

All of a sudden, I felt I was not sitting in front of accomplished sophisticated professionals, but extremely conservative people from backward rustic villages. Yes, in a way they were preserving ancient cultural traditions. They were treating their daughter like a commodity. It was so all so familiar...

I looked at the frenzied melodrama, the overwrought histrionics, convulsing across their faces—and shook my head. If their daughter married an art professor, five thousand years of Indian civilization would instantly collapse. To everyone's amazement, I laughed.

The next time Reena came in for a session, she laughed too. It was then that I knew she would be all right. The conference—well, that quickly turned into complete chaos as all the crowd began chiming in all at once about what Reena should do and how she should live. A dozen cooks, bleating out three dozen different recipes.

Carter sat there with a completely passive expression marred only by an occasional raised eyebrow as things got even more out of hand. It was micromanagement by too many managers on a grand scale, and after a while it got so obviously silly that even Reena could not take it seriously.

Bad enough that her parents should dictate how she should live, but to have the whole squabbling community dictate in person simply bordered on the ridiculous.

"So that's Indian civilization," said Carter to me afterwards. "Gee. I think I need to watch more Bollywood."

By no means did the pressure from Reena's parents come to an end. But its fundamental impotence had been revealed. I don't ascribe it just to that meeting. I ascribe it to Reena's courage and honesty. To her willingness to clarify what she actually believed in our conversations, and then to critically examine those beliefs.

Yes, her parents loved her, raised her, clothed and fed and educated her. Did that give them the power to dictate whom she could love? The simple fact was no. She felt what she felt. No one could dictate that, not even Reena herself.

Did her parents have the power to tell her whom she could marry? They certainly did not have the power. That was Reena's decision. Did she really want to marry a surgeon she did not know, as opposed to someone she loved and had been living with for years? Obviously not.

In psychological terms, Reena was traveling the road from being someone other-directed to becoming someone inner-directed—self-directed. She was learning to understand who she actually was and what she actually wanted. That can be a long journey—a lifetime journey that all of us have to take if we want to achieve genuine individuality.

Reena had taken the first steps. Her progress was visible. Less drinking, less verbal self-abuse, less concealment, less impossible perfectionism.

Slowly Reena became more and more self-aware and self-confident, letting go of many of the unrealistic expectations imposed on by her model minority culture and her controlling parents. She began living up to her own self-set life criteria, not theirs, and yet without mindlessly rebelling against her parents' and culture's standards either. Rather, she began to *weigh* those standards, taking what was of value and setting aside what was not. At least, not valuable for her.

She became less critical of herself, letting go of rules and obsessions over an unattainable 'perfection,' and accepting herself, minor imperfections and all.

Reena believed she was "defaming" her community through her relationship with Carter, but Carter offered her a sense of comfort and care, a non-judgmental acceptance that she'd craved all her life. He made her feel safe and secure, walked with her at her own pace, and provided her with the love and affection needed to heal her injured self.

Had his presence kept her alive during the worst of her extreme guilt-laden self-destructive behavior? Probably. But she had learned not to let gratitude alone dictate her actions. She wanted to be with Carter because she enjoyed being with Carter, not because she owed him anything. It was a choice coming from within her, not a directive being imposed upon her.

And how did it all work out? Quite well.

Reena and Carter got married. Her father was furious, her mother was appalled; the extended family that made up the Indian elite community was shocked, shocked!

But soon her parents began to miss her, and, slowly but surely, began to reconnect. A grandchild sealed the reconciliation. Family, after all, is family.

As for the extended community, they got over it surprisingly quickly, as newer things to gossip about and newer happenings swam into view.

(Besides, Carter proved unexpectedly charming, and a good person to consult regarding art acquisitions.)

Indian civilization? It did not collapse. Somehow Indian culture too managed to endure, even today.

Professionally, Reena returned to her law office but soon began to trying to find a way to reconcile her legal skills with her interests in art. It was not as hard as she thought—there are entire corporations and institutions built around art. It turned out that museums, universities, multimillion-dollar auction transactions, government cultural institutions, all could use the assistance of a Harvard Law School on occasion.

Reena now lives the very life her parents demanded: a life of high eminence, fiscal success, and stellar achievement.

But on her own terms, in her own way, and in areas of her own choosing.

She has become... happy.


And as for me? With Reena's help—and through my experience with other clients, true—I had learned how better to do therapy. Not theoretical book therapy, nor clinical therapy, but real-world, real-life, private practice therapy, with all its twists, uncertainties, personal conflicts, necessary self-discipline, and compassion, all its ambiguities, risks, and surprises.

I had learned what to expect—namely, the unexpected! I had learned to try to analyze dispassionately and without prejudice, and to empathize without illusion or excess sentiment.

But most of all I finally learned to seek that rare critical moment of near-oneness with clients is what I have come to call *attunement*.

It's a phenomenon I have not heard much discussed, but I've learned the importance of seeking it, always, and first and foremost.

I imagine that actors know such 'attunement' when they become so absorbed in the parts, they play that there seems to be no space between themselves and their roles; when the two become as one, *and yet* a certain disciplined separation remains.

The therapist knows this moment of interpersonal near-union too, but between two real persons, not between a real person and a fictional one.

When client and therapist are *attuned,* they have arrived at a point of mutual emotional understanding that nonetheless preserves their respective sense of self.

The client has come to *know* the therapist well enough to let their most critical personal issues stand completely revealed, and to trust the therapist's guidance. The therapist has come to *know* the client well enough, has grown close enough to the client, to see and communicate the best solutions to those difficulties, and lead them out of the dark wood.

Reena and I had so much in common that it was easier for me than it might have otherwise been to reach that area, that attunement. I could *feel* myself standing in her shoes, experiencing her experiences.

Knowing it could be done, I could seek it again, that state; I could strive for it, when treating others.

"At the still point of the turning world," wrote T. S. Eliot, "at the still point, there the dance is." So with therapy. There is a still point in therapy where the soul can know itself, where client and therapist can meet and understand each other.

That is the point from which the therapist can bring the client—and themselves—to a greater spiritual fullness.

## CHAPTER THREE

# CHILD OF THE WIND

The first time I met the woman I'll call 'Maya,' she seemed perfectly pleasant and charming, and the problem she wanted me to help her address was something I felt we could clear up quickly.

I had no idea that she would be returning to me for the next seven years, or still be visiting me today. I certainly never thought that she'd have me seriously reconsidering my aims and ethical boundaries as a therapist, and even what it means to do therapy at all.

Maya was sixty-three years old that first time we met. She was a lecturer at a community college where she taught Gender Identity. She walked into my office with a calm sense of familiarity and of comfort, as if she owned the place. Years of therapy experience in her life seemed to give her a sense of confidence. She carried a large bag and also a small designer purse, along with the take-out lunch she intended to eat during the session.

Maya was a fashion-conscious, rather heavy-set, self-described pansexual, but as charming as a lively mother. Being so comfortable and familiar in a therapist's office, she quickly got to the presenting problem without any formalities of checking in!

"Can I call you Rashmi?" she chirped.

"Of course."

"Since you're much younger!"

"Well..."

"Lovely... you've made it so easy for me... not sure where to begin... I've been in all kinds of therapy all my life. I was an inpatient three times. I tried to commit suicide twice. Once when my weight dropped to a hundred pounds... My mother was a devout Catholic, bless her soul."

(She looked up and made the sign of the cross in front of her chest with a smirk.)

"She absolutely disowned me when I came out as gay"!

I listened intently, nodded, and tried not to look surprised as she went on. I noticed how she was trying to turn our first meeting into more of a simple chit-chat than an initial evaluation.

"Well, we'll discuss my colorful life history over several other sessions," she said. "I've got really *great* insurance!"

She laughed again.

"So," I said, "why are you here?"

"I'm here because I'm madly in love"!

She put her face in her hands and broke down and started sobbing.

It was a simple problem. She was in love, and her love was not returned. Love is not a mental illness, of course, and neither is unrequited love. The first is a wonderful part of the human condition, the second a poignant one, but we have all felt both and lived with them.

Maya's presenting problem was more specific. Her desire was spilling into obsession, and the lack of response from her love object was making her furious and manic.

Maya was a college teacher, and she had fallen in love or rather fallen into an obsession with a twenty-one-year-old student of hers named Nora.

Nora was an attractive Middle Eastern female who believed in being curious about her own sexuality, and she openly talked about it during class discussion. As they both shared the concept of open sexuality, Nora grew closer to Maya. But Nora's interest was intellectual, at least as far as Maya was concerned. Nora wasn't interested in a romantic or physical relationship.

As both their feelings were made clear, the teacher-student relationship became clumsier.

Neither wanted to end it. But unfortunately for Maya, her thoughts had fastened onto Nora with a singleness that began to look like OCD—obsessive-compulsive disorder. Maya would think about Nora from morning till night. She would engage in long inner conversations with Nora. She would have erotic fantasies involving Nora. She would speculate about what Nora was doing and with whom Nora was doing it.

Maya would fly into emotional highs as she imagined idyllic outcomes to their relationship, and crash into severe depression as she berated herself, dwelling on her age and body image and imagined lack of attractiveness. She had only so much mental space in a day, and thoughts of Nora were threatening to take up all of it, crowding out the remainder of her life.

Obsessive thoughts can cause a great deal of pain and inconvenience, but they're by no means an impossible challenge for a therapist with a background in cognitive-behavioral therapy. I was very confident I could help. Such disordered thinking was a challenge handled many times by therapists of the Aaron Beck school, and I knew and admired Beck's valuable work. More than that: I was privileged to have had many opportunities to see and interact with him in person at various CBT and APA conventions.

Beck believed that thoughts, feelings, and behavior were causally linked together: unrealistic thoughts led to painful emotions, which led to maladaptive actions, which resulted in increasingly negative thoughts, which led to even more anxiety, which led to even more self-destructive behavior, and so on and so on. This negative thought loop keeps circulating in our minds, creating a vicious obsessive pattern.

The good news about this unhappy circularity, according to Beck, is that obsessive thinking could be interrupted at any of its points. All you needed to do was have the sufferer pay some mindful and dispassionate attention to their thoughts, and ask:

*Is this thought really true?*

*Is the way I am looking at things now realistic, or silly?*

*Is there another way of looking at things?*

*A better way?*

You could also have them undertake behavioral assignments. It's hard to let your thoughts wander down dark avenues when the mind occupied in a task that needed attention and focus. Nor did assignments have to be rigorous or daunting. (Riding a roller coaster or a turn skiing downhill concentrates the mind wonderfully!)

Maya greatly enjoyed our sessions in which she described her fantasies involving Nora. She enjoyed them a little too greatly—she was using our sessions to feed her obsessive focus on Nora. The trick was to get her to *observe* those fantasies, not just wallow in them.

As I eased her in that direction, slowly Maya and I began looking at the thoughts she was thinking less emotionally, and evaluating them more objectively. We began to set goals for activities that would direct her thinking to more positive objects, and away from her constant self-deprecation and her focus on Nora.

In the therapeutic world, this sort of approach comes in the inedible form of numb coma-inducing technical terminology—metacognition, behavioral intervention, schema monitoring, cognitive restructuring, and so on. (For those interested, works by the psychologist Albert Ellis on rational-behavior therapy puts much of the approach across clearly, but in a blunt salty manner.)

In actual practice with a client, however, the technique is much more concrete. I would simply ask Maya what exactly she was thinking, and she would tell me. Sometimes I would ask her to write her thoughts down when not in a session, and she did. Then, together, we would examine them, and (like most maladaptive thinking) a little mindful examination would put them in perspective and reduce their hold.

"What if she *leaves* me?" she would moan.

"Has she said she plans to leave you? I thought you told me she wanted to continue with you as her teacher."

"That's true... but if she *does* leave, I *can't live without her!*"

"Didn't you live without her before you met her?"

"Well... yes... "

Were you miserable then?"

"Well... no... "

"How would you feel if you *could* live without her?"

"I can't!"

"Imagine that you could. Pretend. For instance, can you just say the words, "I can live without her"? Try. They're only words, after all."

It's important to remember that a therapist should not *attack* a client's maladaptive thinking. The goal is to guide the patient to examine their *own* thinking, but to do so mindfully and dispassionately. If the thoughts are genuinely negative and harmful, their inaccuracy and extremism soon become clear. Better thoughts—better maps of reality—follow.

We often fail to notice the impact of such thoughts because a good deal of our thinking is automatic, or because thoughts slip in sub-vocally under the cover of unexamined assumptions. Faced directly, and in the light of reason, however, a good deal of the unnecessary intensity—and sometimes silliness—of our unexamined thinking is released.

So it was with Maya. Yes, Maya was in love—but conceded that she had been in love before (many times) and survived. Yes, she loved Nora—but she did have to admit too that Nora was not perfect in every possible way, and that a diet of weeping over Nora every moment of the day not only failed to bring her any closer to Nora, but was as fatiguing as it was unproductive.

She conceded that the teacher-student relation they had had gave her pleasure and worked for them both, whereas a torrid drama-filled affair might not be as much of a pleasure in reality as in fantasy.

Slowly, Nora began to assume again the human dimensions of a friend, rather than the heated image of a love object. And the important thing to remember is that this new perspective was not a collection of thoughts and feelings I *imposed* on Maya; they were ideas that came to Maya spontaneously as she and I discussed her situation from a realistic and not an emotionally overheated angle.

Behavioral assignments were part of Maya's

therapy too, and they were easy to give. Maya had an amazing range of interests, and she was naturally talented. She liked to paint, for instance, and when she painted, she would fall almost into a kind of trance. Thoughts of Nora would fall away. So, not surprisingly, I assigned her to paint! At least part of her day would be happily spent, and Nora-free. Her teaching offered a similar release. The more attention she gave to her other students, the less the exclusive focus on Nora.

It's quite amazing how even a small amount of mindful attention to one's thoughts, how even a brief and tiny amount of redirection to other reinforcing thoughts and activities, can moderate toxic obsessive thinking.

Soon Maya's obsessive intoxication passed from being continual to being occasional to not being bothersome at all.

But that was not the end of Maya's appearances in my office. Far from it.

Soon she was there again. This time a financial problem was causing her anguish. As with Nora, it was once again the end of the world. How would she ever cope!

And when that was resolved, it was a family problem.

And when *that* was resolved, it was something else.

Did any of her problems rise to the level of serious mental illness? Happily, no.

But did she experience emotional pain and anxiety? Sadly, yes.

Did any of these problems leave her incapacitated? No. She would have issues with family and friends, financial issues, work issues, tax issues. Most of all, she admitted, she suffered from *loneliness*, a deep corrosive loneliness that now and again threatened to sink her into a deep depression.

But she was far from being a clinical depressive. With a little self-examination, a little help, a little reflection, a few visits, she would bob back up, feisty and vital as ever.

I am not a Freudian, but there was a touch of the Freudian about her ups and downs: it did seem to me very likely that her individual crises were the symptoms of a greater underlying problem. Often that sort of deeper underlying issue has deep roots, so Maya and I began to stray from the specifics of her complaints and began talking about her upbringing and her childhood.

It was not a happy story. Maya had been sexually abused by her cousin as a child. Her parents, products of the Sixties hippie culture, were oblivious. To hear Maya tell it, they were oblivious to a great deal more than that, for drugs and drift were a part of the family lifestyle for as long as she could remember. Her parents raised her with no boundaries, no expectations, no direction; although they *did* manage *to* introduce her to marijuana, which became a frequent and lifelong companion.

As an adult, Maya took pride in her upbringing as an immature, irresponsible 'child of the wind.' Cool sober analysis was not for Maya. When we discussed problem solving in therapy, she'd often cry out, " I'm a big cry-baby!" and literally cry.

As Maya grew older, she too, like her parents, began to drift. Her adolescence was a series of house parties where she, along with everyone else, was quite stoned. There, in a haze, she found herself introduced to sexual practices and partners of all sorts, engaging with everything through the haze of drink and pot. She began thinking of herself as a lesbian, but her partners were by no means limited to women. Nor were there any lasting connections, whatever the gender. Her romantic life, like the rest of her life, became a matter of immediate impulse.

*But,* it was by no means an unpleasant life. Merely a very disorderly one. Maya lived like a butterfly. She floated from blossom to blossom. She had no overarching personal or professional goals. She would consistently pursue immediate short-term gratifications over long-term rewards.

But they *were* gratifying. She had had many good times. Now in her sixties, she was still having a rather good time. She was by no means an unhappy person, or even a dysfunctional one. She had gotten a college degree in some subject in the humanities and drifted into a clerical job at a bank. She didn't like it. It required responsibility and long hours, and commitment was always a struggle for Maya. So she went back to school, this time for a doctorate in Education. The long hours and brutal discipline of graduate school were not for Maya either. She survived for three years and then quit.

With no regular source of income and no motivation to work, she went home to live with her elderly father who needed care. At this point her mother passed away, and at some point after that she went from being a care-giver only for her father to being a care-giver for others. She began calling herself a healer, and offered a somewhat woozy blur of meditation and yoga and Art Therapy classes at the local park district.

It was not carefully thought out, but it did hearten and comfort people. She helped others, supported herself, drifted in and out of relationships, and—enjoyed life. She even got on famously now with her cousin who had abused her! It was an existence that seemed equal parts incoherence and *joie de vivre.* But her enjoyment of it was evident in her face and manner and was no small part of her charm.

And, strange to say, this contradiction became the source for a good deal of reflection on my own part about the task of therapy and the therapist's role.

Sometimes outsiders see therapy in almost robo-mechanical terms. A sick person goes to a psychiatrist or therapist much like a car goes to a garage for maintenance and repair. The patient has some problem, and the therapist is there to 'fix' the problem, fast, and send them on their merry way. A few therapists fall into this mindset too, especially therapists wedded to one single school or theory: they try to impose their own idea of what a well-functioning person should be onto the patient, subtly pressuring and manipulating them into something they do not want to be.

But this is the opposite of acceptance, of individuation. A patient needs to develop into *who they are*, the identity that has always been uniquely theirs, but that is too often distorted by pressure from family and environment and society to make them fit into roles they never wanted or chose.

This was my problem with Maya. Yes, her life was chaotic—but she *liked* chaos. She was very happy with her life of drift and impulse and immediate gratification. She always had been. True, there were frequent bumps along the way, but the bumps weren't devastating, or at least not enough to motivate a change of lifestyle. She simply needed a shoulder to cry on now and then, a sympathetic ear, a bit support, someone to be there for her to help her weather the *small* storms of her life. Overall, she was rather content with being tossed along on the wings of the wind.

After working with so many high achievers and workaholics in my practice, my deepening understanding of Maya took me almost by surprise. Her life might seem to *me* disorderly, but to her it was free and rich and entertaining.

As I came to understand the *kind* of care she wanted, I was able to provide it. Yet my approach with Maya was not exactly therapy as I had earlier thought of it—I was not uncovering and resolving deep-seated issues that were causing a client intense pain or disrupting their lives intolerably. But I *was* providing healing and necessary support that visibly did my client good.

Did I want Maya to live a more orderly and consistent life? I did. I like to think that I succeeded—that I added at least a little more order and consistency to her stormy lifestyle. She needed that badly, and knew it, and wanted it—but not *too* much of it.

Working with Maya helped me to realize that a good therapist works with the *grain* of a patient, as it were; that the goal of therapy is not change for efficiency's sake so much as for the sake of self-realization. The task of a therapist is to resolve the client's problems as the *client* understands them. A therapist's skill lies in helping them deepen their understanding of that problem, helping them expand the range of the solutions they consider.

And those things matter. But thanks to Maya, I began to realize that ultimately, I was there to help my clients achieve *their* goals, not my own.

True, part of that involved helping the client to better understand those goals. As they grew in self-insight, they might even find themselves modifying those goals.

But it was the client who had to lead the way.

The sculptor Michelangelo once said that the sculpture he was creating was already there in the marble: the blows of his chisel did not shape a blank block of stone, they liberated a form that was already there.

This is the job of the therapist: to release an individuality that is already there, to remove the blocks preventing it from emerging.

But how? For me, the key element in therapy

has proven to be *empathy*. Successful therapy begins with seeing a client's life through a client's eyes. But *empathy* is not *sympathy*. Sympathy is valuable, certainly. But one can *sympathize* with the suffering of others without having any deep understanding of what they're experiencing or why, much less having any inspired insight as to the best way to resolve that problem. *Empathy* allows you to experience the client's situation imaginatively, from the inside. One provides support, but support from within the perspective of the patient, not from outside.

Maya helped me to understand that *pure* empathy—meeting the client on their own terms, seeing their perspective for within, accepting their own goals for what they were—was not enough. To genuinely help the client, what was needed was *structured empathy*, a kind of 'designer strategy' where classic cognitive-behavioral techniques more closely conformed to the client's *clarified* goals and *deep* individuality.

Maya wanted to *embrace* her drift, and there was nothing I could, or should, have done about it. But at the same time, she didn't want to drift so far that she would strike the rocks, crash, and sink. There I could help and did.

Maya remains a client to this day. Nora has gone, replaced by other (lesser) Noras. Maya's ups and downs continue to rise and fall—but they don't shoot her up so far that she might fall and hurt herself, nor fall so far as to even approach clinical depression.

Maya continues to live her life as she has always

lived it—she rarely misses her weekly sessions with me, and I find her as charming as ever. Sometimes Maya is a drama queen narrating stories in which the entire world is against her; at other times she's problem-solving in a sincere straightforward effective manner. Over the years our therapeutic relationship has become a strong personal bond and I always look forward to our delightful sessions.

Are they a little *too* delightful? In some ways. We have become (and remain) friends. She texts me images constantly of her travels and brings me gifts that I cannot accept. She'll offer to treat me for lunch, call me for dinner, invite me to her parties. It's very tempting to go. Maya is a great deal of fun.

But each time I remind her—and myself—that there is a line past which the therapist and his or her client cannot and should not cross. It is a soft line, not hard and fast, and a grey line, not perfectly clear. But there are boundaries in that apparent freedom, boundaries that make that freedom possible.

That's yet another way that Maya (like so many of my clients) has become *my* teacher, and I her student.

## CHAPTER FOUR

# THE ICEBERG

Media often portray Post-Traumatic Stress Disorder as something that only afflicts soldiers, a personal cataclysm that leaves them shattered and helpless.

In fact, its more common victims are children; and enduring trauma may lie underneath even the most polished surface of the highest achievers.

The client I'll call 'Michael' was one such case, and one such high achiever.

Michael had it all. He was an eminent, wealthy, well-regarded, and extremely successful neurosurgeon.

He was trained at and employed by an Ivy League Medical School.

He had an attractive wife, and four children on their way to the best schools.

He was respected, honored, and envied. He didn't come to me because he felt he needed my help. He was the sort of person who looked as though he needed help and support from no one; particularly not his wife, Sarah, who was my initial client.

Sarah was referred to me from a local hospital inpatient program where she was admitted for apparent suicidal thoughts and depression. The psychiatrist briefly oriented me concerning her condition prior to my first appointment. It seemed not uncommon—yet another case of depression stemming from the overwhelming stress of a home to manage, a busy husband, and a hyperkinetic bevy of young children.

Sarah described herself as sad and resigned in the initial session. It was hard for her to regulate her emotions, she said. She was already on anti-depressants and sleep medication. She frequently broke down in tears.

"How often do you feel depressed?" I asked.

"Most of the time, Dr. Pandey." she said.

"Why?" I asked.

Her lip curled.

"Why do you *think?* Who *wouldn't* be depressed living around Michael?"

She almost spat the name. Clearly it would not take a great deal of time unearthing her particular problem: Sarah was not at all happy in her marriage. She was especially not happy with her husband, Michael.

They had been married sixteen years, and yet Sarah felt that Michael regarded her with contempt, a superior contempt that he directed coolly and evenly to virtually everyone. They had not married for love: their union had been an Old-World union—a matchmaker's arrangement pressed on both through their families.

But it was a good match, the families agreed. Michael's father was himself a well-regarded physician, and Michael was set to follow in his footsteps. His wife-to-be's family belonged to the medical community in New York. Both families believed it would be a good and fruitful union. In some ways it was. Four children soon came along, and Michael's professional eminence and the family's assets seemed to only grow and prosper.

From outside, the marriage seemed rather a success—yet another triumphant entry in Michael's continuing string of accomplishments.

From inside, it was anything but.

"He's an iceberg. An *iceberg*," said Sarah. *Hissed* Sarah. "I can't *stand* him any longer. He's so *cold*. He never opens up. Never! He doesn't smile, he doesn't relax, he doesn't talk to me. He doesn't *care*."

Therapists learn to be sensitive to how clients use words. The way Sarah put her barb, cracking it like a whip, would catch any therapist's attention. Only a tenth of an iceberg is seen above water, as we all know. Nine-tenths is hidden.

Was she only saying that Michael's interest in her had waned, as passions sometime do in a marriage, or that there was a deeper problem going on in Michael than was apparent?

I played Devil's Advocate. Sarah was certainly an intelligent woman, the possessor of an MBA in her own right. But she didn't share Michael's intense focus on professional eminence. She herself had made no professional mark. Was she saying that she resented Michael for enjoying such professional success?

She waved her hand. No, no, no. Raising four children, even with the help of a governess, was profession enough for Sarah, and meaningful enough.

What rankled was Michael's sheer intolerable *coldness*. His attention was absorbed entirely in his work, she said, and in his determination to outperform others. He acted as though he regarded her degree, her interests, her conversation, her presence as boring and irritating. According to Sarah, he treated everyone that way. He was a dutiful enough father, but not, she said, a particularly loving or interested one. His life was not his family: it was his work, and in his mind his work consisted of outperforming the competition. He did so briskly, brilliantly, efficiently—and quietly despised his less accomplished peers and colleagues and staff.

As the sessions progressed, I began to feel that Sarah's depression was mostly a matter of asphyxiation—of living a relationship devoid of mutual affection or respect. Michael was not abusive in any crude sense, although he berated her often about spending the money he had earned, and minor disagreements would quickly burn with acid sarcasm. Yet he acted with no deliberate cruelty: Michael was the provider, and he did what a good husband and father was expected to do—provide. The problem was only that he did it with indifference—worse, with disdain, an emotion that he lavished over everything but his own preening narcissism.

Of course, that was *her* view of things. And I gave very close and sympathetic attention to those views. The happiness or unhappiness of a person, their picture of their situation, is always true *for them*. But that picture is not always the whole one.

Our feelings color and filter our perceptions, and our interpretations can be misinterpretations. Clearly, she felt the problem in her marriage was Michael, but I couldn't assume Michael was the villain. I had had too much experience working with patients to reduce anyone to that sort of caricature. Whatever the truth of the situation, Michael was the person I needed to speak to in order to learn more.

So, I asked her if her husband would be willing to come in for a talk. If he was as she described him, I wanted to learn more about what drove him to act and feel as he did.

She was not hopeful. She believed that he didn't believe in therapy; moreover, she felt he would have trust issues about discussing his personal concerns with a stranger, and especially not in front of her. She declined even to ask. The suggestion would only leave her further humiliated.

With her consent, I offered to email Michael myself, and invite him to a one-on-one session without her present, purely to gain further insight into Sarah's current emotional state. Like Sarah, I wasn't hopeful he would agree. But why not try?

To my surprise, she consented, and I sent Michael my invitation

To my further surprise, he not only read and responded immediately, but offered to come in as early as I could accommodate him.

I saw a ray of hope. Perhaps it *was* possible salvage their relationship.

Michael set strict conditions, however. The session should not last more than an hour, and Michael would only see me by himself. He stated flatly that he was not interested in couples therapy, or in reaching any sort of new 'emotional 'understanding' between himself and Sarah, or attending marital sessions involving them both. Sarah's therapy was Sarah's therapy.

Why come, then? He may not have been interested, but my impending first session with Michael certainly interested me.

"The client is here, Dr. Pandey," said my secretary.

"Please let him in," I said.

I put my paperwork aside, and Michael entered my office.

He was exceptionally well-dressed, groomed and manicured. He chose a chair and sat with an air of confidence and yet suspicion, looking around with a tight-lipped expression and hawk-like eyes, his features at once intense and disdainful.

His body language was not easy to read. But he was not the monster that Sarah had been painting. Michael was respectful and cautious in his choice of words, yet guarded. He clearly wanted to say something, yet wanted not to say it. He said that he assumed I had written him in order 'to help Sarah with her issues,' but left it there: he didn't describe those issues as he saw them, nor did he offer much help. He volunteered almost no new information, and said even less about his own perspective on those issues. Mostly he responded to questions, and to those he responded briefly.

How did he see the current situation at home generally, I asked? He said that Sarah's emotional state made no sense to him. Everything was fine at home. *Everything.*

Sarah painted a very different picture. But—as per my rule—I couldn't share my conversation with Sarah in the session.

It was frustrating and a little puzzling. Why had he even come if he was going to provide so very little? All too soon the hour was up, and all I could do was thank him for his time. So I thanked him for his time, and he got up to leave.

But as he got up to leave, he hesitated.

"Doctor... is it all right for me to come see you personally—for my own individual sessions?"

Again, there were conditions. He wanted to meet with me regularly for another six weeks. He presented it as another of his many projects—an experiment that he would judge by its results, to be discontinued if it no longer seemed to be worth his time.

I had learned almost nothing about him during our session together, and if every session we were to have resembled this one, not much would get accomplished.

Nonetheless, for no reason I could articulate, I agreed.

Not long afterwards Sarah's depression seemed to lessen. Soon she felt better enough to discontinue our talks, though she continued to stay in touch with me by phone and email for months afterwards.

As for Michael?

The cool and distant neurosurgeon visited me regularly for the next three years. Often dissolving into execration, explosions of fury, and tears.

Michael passed along his story slowly, and in bits and chunks. He was the only son of immigrant parents. But his parents were a very special sort of immigrant. They were Polish Jews who had somehow managed to escape their nation during the apocalyptic years of World War Two.

I never knew them except through Michael's descriptions them and so cannot speak to their own traumas. I do understand that there is a qualitative difference between facing one's personal death, even in war, and living under the shadow of Holocaust: of the mass extermination, the possible extinction, of your entire people. I learned that those years darkened them, and Michael's father and mother reacted very differently to that darkness.

Michael's father forcibly put his internal crises aside. He became the prototype for his son: he gave himself entirely to his profession. He was a physician, and he gave himself over completely to becoming an excellent and successful one, supporting his family financially but distancing himself emotionally. To Michael, he became a paradigm:

the model for how a husband, a father, and a man should act. A man should devote himself wholly to his profession and excel at it. Parenting was not unimportant, but, like other considerations, it was secondary. Less than secondary. A father's duty was to provide whatever externals a child like Michael needed. Emotional needs were left to Michael's mother.

And that was the tragedy; for his mother was not emotionally stable. Not at all. I am positive if she were treated today she would be diagnosed with extreme paranoid schizophrenia. Less clinically: Michael's mother was insane.

Michael's childhood was marred thoughout by his mother's manic actions, fits and incidents that filled his days with terror. He had no understanding of his mother's turbulent behavior, her crying episodes, her regular meltdowns. The chaos she engendered became the norm for him, and he began spending all his time locked in his room with his books, his fear and his loneliness.

It took several sessions to gain enough trust for Michael to truly open up, and when opened up, he immediately broke down.

It was during a session in which he brought up the subject of Post-Traumatic Stress Disorder, and asked about the persistent effects of past trauma on an individual's present life.

We discussed the subject in the abstract for a moment, and then I tried to bring the discussion back around to his childhood experiences.

"How would you describe your childhood relationships with your parents?" I asked. "With your mother?

Michael's face became red as he looked down to the floor.

To my shock, he was fighting tears. Trembling.

I thought he was too proud, too self-contained, to break down like this in my office. But he was unable to control the torrent of emotions.

"Mom was crazy.... just *absolutely crazy*... DSM textbook insane. She tried to kill me twice. She nearly did."

I nodded. It was impossible to look at his face, formerly so cold, and not feel compassion.

"Go on."

"I was seven years old in second grade. I had a spelling test that mom helped me prepare for. I was afraid I wouldn't do well. I hated spelling. That's when it happened. I didn't do well. I got a C on the test.

"Mother was furious. *Livid.* When she found out she screamed at me to go to my room. I was hungry and tired, and I needed someone to tell me... to tell me that it was *okay,* that, that, I'd do great next time. I asked her to stop screaming at me. She started hitting me instead. Hitting me and slapping me.

"I ran to my room and locked the door. I wanted to avoid another round of her slapping me and kicking me. After an hour, I slowly opened the door. I wanted to go to kitchen to get some cookies.

"There she was. Standing there with a butcher knife. She *screamed* and *came at me...*"

Michael was sobbing into his hands at this point.

Quietly I passed the tissue box closer to him.

"I'm sorry," said Michael, the tears running down his cheeks.

I nodded. "Please go on."

"I froze. I *froze!* She *lunged* at me with the knife! I screamed so loud... I turned and ran, I didn't know where I was going, but I opened the front door and I ran out into the streets. I didn't care if the neighbors saw me. I ran, and I kept running, and screaming. "She's going to kill me! *She's going to kill me!*

"The next-door neighbor was a man called Mr. Smith. He was mowing his lawn. He saw me and he stopped me. He took me inside his house and tried to calm me down. I was shaking. Waves of shame and fear were washing over me at the same time.

"'Why are you screaming, boy?' he asked me. 'What's going on? Exactly who is going to kill you.''

"I just kept crying. I couldn't say anything at all. Mrs. Smith came out and gave me some food. She asked if she should call my mom.

"I screamed at her '*No! Don't!*'

"I didn't know what to do. I just kept sitting there. They comforted me, and offered to walk me home. I was a child, I didn't know what to do. Should I tell them about my crazy mom? Should I keep quiet?

"Right then the doorbell rang. It was my dad. My dad had come to pick me up."

After that session, the floodgates opened. In next few sessions Michael described incident after awful incident. Sometimes he'd request two-hour sessions. His entire body would shake as he vividly relived devastatingly painful moments—moments of emotional and not only emotional torture. Clearly, he grew up terrified.

Time and time again, he said, Michael's father would intervene to save the boy. And yet it was also the father who ultimately kept the boy's torture going. The father tried to act with a degree of humanity to both wife and son. He refused to have his wife committed, and she was never under guard or institutional care till elderly. Within those limits Michael's father nonetheless took such care of the boy as he could. Uncontrollably violent fits were infrequent, and there were signals indicating that her rages were coming, signals that allowed Michael's father to shield his son from the worst.

But not always. Time and again there would be 'incidents' that never quite rose to the level of institutionalization or arrest.

Michael survived them, up until such time as he could be put in a private school.

There he excelled. He was a model pupil—lest he be expelled and have to go back home. As for Michael's father, he might be physically and emotionally distant from Michael, but not as an example. Michael became driven to follow in his father's footsteps—to follow in them, and so to escape.

Michael rose to the top of his class, and then to the top of his college classes, then to the top of his profession, and then, because it was expected and it was a mark of success, a marriage was arranged and children of his own followed.

Again, he acted like his model, his father. He was

a dutiful provider who preferred to be elsewhere; a superlative surgeon who had no interest in his patients as people; a leading medical professional who regarded peers and colleagues as inferior competitors meriting only his contempt. He had no close friends, anyone to whom to unburden himself. He had no romantic relationships, in marriage or out. He took little joy in anything, it seemed, except for hitting and exceeding his professional goals.

As he initially bragged of his accomplishments, and strenuously avoided discussing his inner life, I thought of the title of T.S. Eliot's poem, *The Hollow Man*. I had come to know the sadness and pain of his childhood. But that was then. He was a man now. An adult. What was going on in his mind and emotions now? What was *inside* this highly accomplished, utterly alone, individual?

Slowly he began to open up and show me; to tell me the story of his life. Perhaps it was the first time he had ever shared it with anyone.

The therapeutic situation is paradoxical. People imagine that it follows a medical model in which the therapist assigns some sorts of behavioral practices or applies a drug and improvement is imposed from without.

But the truth is that people who have in some way been crippled by circumstances have a natural drive to achieve the wholeness that was their birthright. A broken limb wants naturally to heal; it only needs to be properly set.

So it is with a broken mind. What is bent within

us wants naturally to straighten. The question is how to clear away the obstacles that still block that self-healing process.

In Michael's case the core emotion, the core obstacle, was a fundamental loneliness—a lifelong lack of anyone to whom to communicate emotionally. He turned away from those areas he could not deal with, to focus outwards on the material success where he excelled. But there is no flight from self and memory. The prisoner carries his prison within him.

There is a story I once heard about two Hindu monks. Both are walking beside a river to a monastery, when, on the bank of the river, they see a woman. She needs desperately to cross the river, but is afraid she'll be unable to resist the strong current.

The older of the monks, seeing her distress, picks her up, wades across the river with the woman in his arms, puts her on the other bank, and then returns to his brother monk to continue their journey.

The two monks walk along in silence.

Finally the younger monk turns and shouts.

"How could you *possibly* touch a woman? We are *monks*. We have taken a sacred vow to Brahma to *never approach* a woman, much less touch a woman's body. Yet you pick up a woman and hold her in your arms and carry her across the river as though it means nothing at all!"

"I picked up someone in need, and when we reached the other side of the river, I put her down," said the older monk. "You are still carrying her."

So was Michael. So it is with PTSD in general. It's not so much that a terrifying incident happens. It's that people like Michael return to such incidents over and over, reliving them. Michael had not grown up, had not progressed at all. Fifty years had gone by, but not a day passed that Michael would not go back and relive some episode of horror. He could not let those memories go, nor did he even try to come to terms with them. Like the young monk, he continued to carry them in his mind, and so condemned himself to reliving them all his life.

His father too had never confronted the dysfunctional nature of his family's life—he too sought only to keep it under control. Once more Michael followed the model set by his father: intellectually he realized the abnormality of his upbringing, the strange isolation of his personal relation to others.

But intellect alone—like emotion alone—isn't enough to produce emotional wholeness.

And was that, in fact, why Michael had asked to see me? The therapist stands in a complex relationship to a client: he or she is there to help them solve *their* perceived problem, not to reshape them in whatever way the therapist might think is better for them. Michael, quite frankly, showed no interest in getting along better with his wife. He was clearly lonely, but at the same time stated flatly and sincerely that he was uninterested in and disdainful of others. His problem was simply that he was *miserable,* chronically unhappy, and did not know why.

That particular problem was not hard to solve.

It was a matter of obsessive thinking. He was miserable because every day he would repeatedly re-live miserable moments from his past.

People imagine that re-living a painful moment from one's past is by itself therapeutic. That's not the case. Re-living painful memories over and over again is like hearing the same song on the radio over and over. It may bring back old feelings but there is no emotional development, no emotional progress. There is no emotional progress because the person re-living the memory fails to re-live that moment with *understanding*, to revisit it *mindfully.*

The person re-living the memory also generally has poor attentional skills and habits: he or she has not learned to redirect their attention to more supportive topics, or to use the appearance of a negative thought as a *trigger* to spark more supportive thoughts or recollections, to envision solutions and resolutions.

Together, this is what Michael and I began to do. It was not a learning journey that could be completed overnight, certainly. Years were needed. Years and no small amount of courage. Simple training was not enough: Michael needed to face the memories he would learn to handle in a new way, and, to be sure, those memories hurt.

So, our sessions together proceeded slowly. I approached our first talks together by framing them in a way Michael had perhaps never experienced. I gave him an open space without condemnation in which he could look at himself and into his own situation—now, in the present moment—

and simply share whatever he wished to share.

For all his narcissism, he nonetheless retained a basic realism of a medical training. He knew, soberly, that his marriage was not working, that his relation to his children was a repetition of the cold distance he had known unhappily with his father, that something in his inner life was wrong.

After a few jabs of perfunctory sarcasm, of asserting his elevated status, of faulting his wife, the façade began cracking. He began to talk; and to talk to someone who was not sitting in judgment on him, someone with whom he was not in competition, someone assisting him to quietly look inward instead ferociously striving outward.

In most people's minds there is a kind of surface chatter in which they make plans, repeat common clichés, complain about pressing issues and immediate problems and so on. But at the same time, under that surface run enduring under-currents—memories and areas of thought to which the mind returns, like a stone sinking to the bottom of a brook.

That was how it was with Michael. He might begin by complaining about his wife's spending, his children's test scores on exams. But soon heavier themes emerged from the depths. Barely a few sessions passed before he began recounting one horror after another in his childhood; and his narcissism, his cool façade, would fall away. The specters of memories that continued to haunt him began to emerge.

At this point I did suggest a behavioral practice.

I suggested that he try the 'Empty Chair' technique.

"What's that?" he said with characteristic suspicion.

"I place an empty chair in front of you. You imagine that someone very important to you is sitting in it. You tell them things—things you may have wanted to say to them all your life."

"That's just nonsense," he softly snarled. "Make-believe."

"You believe in the experimental method, don't you? Try it. See what happens."

"You can't talk to someone who's not there."

"Of course you can. Try. Use your imagination. They can talk to you too," I said.

"No. They *can't.*"

"*Try.* Pick someone. Ask them something. What do you think they'll say? All right, maybe it's not what the person would actually say. But it's what *you* believe they would say. What you believe they would say tells us a great deal about *you*. And we both want to learn more about you. The inner you. The real you."

He tried.

The results were quick, and electric.

*Of course* he wanted to address his mother. *Of course* the composed, controlled, powerful and successful individual was soon screaming abuse and vitriol at an empty chair. *Of course* wild tears soon streamed down his face and across his very expensive tie.

What did I do? Nothing. I became invisible. I informed him beforehand that I was not a participant in his conversations—not a judge, not a guide, not there to mend or even to witness. Only a forgotten presence. A space of acceptance.

And I was ignored very quickly as the monologues went on. But I learned very much.

As a therapist, nothing to me is more amazing than those moments in which a person seems to suddenly and completely transform. Their façade may be cold, or friendly, or intellectual, or resistant, or bored—it doesn't matter. Suddenly an inner line will be crossed, an interior dam break. Out rushes a pent-up storm that carries everything before, that clarifies a wound that will not be acknowledged and has never healed. Till now it stands there plain and unavoidable.

Michael had several such moments. There were things he did not want to re-live, but had never stopped re-living, and would never stop re-living till he saw them plainly for the first time. This, very gradually, he was doing, till, stone by stone, the wall separating him from others slowly began to come down.

People like to imagine that therapy always entails a happy fairy-tale ending that couples always reconcile in the end, that anger always melts into forgiveness. That is not the case. Therapy is about reality: about a person's decision to explore and face his or her own inner truth.

In Michael's case, the truth was that he had never loved his wife and she had never loved him. Neither really wanted reconciliation, only an end to being yoked unwillingly together. Couples therapy was not called for, for they had never been a true couple. As Michael ended his therapy visits, the marriage was dissolving.

But amicably. They had never been as happy with each other as when they were parting. It was an ending that had the promise of a new and better beginning.

Nor did Michael reconcile with his mother. Yes, she was still alive. She continued to live on into her Nineties in an institution for the elderly. Michael had never visited her there. Perhaps he has since, I don't know. I do know that by the time our sessions ended, he no longer hated her blamed her. Is that the same as forgiveness? Possibly, possibly not. But by then he had come to realize, *emotionally*, that her behavior was not a matter of malice or hatred, but of illness. She had no control over herself or her actions.

The anger that had spilled out during his Empty Chair sessions was the pain and anger of a child. Now that he had re-lived and reviewed those experiences as an adult, he could see his mother's terrible unfreedom in its own terms. She was to be pitied.

*Did* he pity her? Did he forgive her? I don't know. But a day came when he said that he no longer hated her, and it had the ring of truth.

One of the joys of my profession is the privilege of seeing people suddenly open up emotionally, like a flower curled up tight in the darkness opening itself up to a ray of sunlight. There is a beauty and inspiration to that moment, the moment when a person faces the truth about their experience and sees their own face for the first time in a new and truer light.

Michael was indeed a high achiever: he aspired not just to professional excellence but to a spiritual excellence. He wanted to be free of his coldness, his anger, his pain. He wanted to understand it, and the reasons for it, and exchange it for a greater wholeness.

Slowly—to a degree—he achieved his goal. His obsessive re-enactments of his terrified childhood petered out. His fear and shame and anger dissipated and dissolved. His past was no longer a theatre of repeated performances, but only a distant and receding record of facts he had no need to revisit. Sad facts, perhaps, but then he had a life to live now, a life with tremendous responsibilities and options. That is the direction toward which he now turned.

His marriage to Sarah was no longer one of those options. But it did not pass away in anger. Both husband and wife had grown enough to see that they had not been brought together by choice, and had not stayed together except because of the expectations of others and the dull weight of habit.

Each partner wanted—and realized that they deserved—something more.

Each wished the other well as they went their own way to seek it.

## CHAPTER FIVE

# POUND OF FLESH

Amy initially came to my practice when she was still in college. She was nineteen. I still remember the way she looked in the waiting room—wide-eyed, in faded jeans, standing there fidgeting in Reeboks, a massive Chicago college logo splashed over her sweatshirt.

She stood up promptly, almost at attention.

"Dr. Pandey?"

"Hi. You're Amy? I'm Dr. Pandey. It's nice to meet you."

Some people approach a therapist's office in embarrassment or distress. Some are desperate, distraught, aching for solutions to abysmal situations, afraid that soon they'll have to bare all their shameful secrets to a complete stranger in the hope of finding an answer.

Not this young lady. She seemed completely at ease in a therapist's office. Even eager.

"Have you been in therapy before, Amy?" I

asked.

"Doc, I've been doing this shit for *years*. My Dad made me go for therapy when I was 5 years old. I would play with Legos and bouncy balls in her office. Sometimes I would sleep for a bit when I was tired. My therapist, Ms. Harvey? She was really nice! "

She paused and stepped over to the window and looked outside and down.

"Look at them all... People go crazy in Chicago during summer... All these tourists... I hate them..."

She laughed and rolled her eyes.

I smiled with her.

"What brings you back to therapy now?" I asked.

"My family. My family is, like, a control-freak squad, y'know? Mostly my dad. He won't let me *breathe*, y'know? Like I'm in *college* now, y'know? I'm supposed to make my *own* decisions! *Duh?*"

She rolled her eyes again. She shifted on the couch. She picked up a pillow and hugged it.

I noticed that Amy was certainly familiar with one aspect of a therapeutic visit: she knew she was seeing someone who would listen to her without a reaction or judgment, so her outburst flowed and flowed, changing swiftly into anger as her voice got louder and more excited. She felt safe to express her feelings, and didn't hesitate for a moment.

Her speech was so manic, in fact, that I suspected she was medicated. I kept listening nonetheless. Not just to her words but to the emotional hues shifting through everything she was saying, to her facial expression, her body language.

I wanted to let her complete her chain of thoughts. I wanted to steer her into the now, and focus her on the present. After she went on a bit more, I cut in.

"So. What's going on now?" I asked.

"My grades are slipping. Well, not all of them. Well, a *lot* of them. But I'm a good student. Like, in High School. I was in Honors classes! I got a scholarship! How many students get that? Not the idiots I sit next to in class now. Oh no. College is *party party party time* for them. *Rich* kids," she sneered. "Their *money*, their *parents*, their *cars.* What bullshit. My sorority sisters are all about Prada and Tiffany and whatnot. Not me! I'm a misfit there, Dr. Pandey: I'm poor. Too poor, too ugly-looking, and too damned *fat!*"

She broke down in tears. Tears of anger, tears of frustration. Tears of self-loathing and shame. Tears of underlying sadness.

I was far from approaching even a hint of diagnosis, but I couldn't ignore the savage self-degradation in the way she said 'fat.' It was like the crack of a whip, a slap in her own face.

Fat—body dysmorphia, we now call it—is a serious medical condition, and an increasingly complicated psychological one. The DSM no longer limits itself to traditional eating disorder categories, i.e., anorexia and bulimia. Now we have, alongside body dysmorphia, names like restrictive diet syndrome, orthorexia, 'over-exercising syndrome' New nomenclatures and terms continue to emerge, in parallel with the numerous fad diets and exercises intended help people lose weight and look attractive. Obesity may well become a civil rights category, as 'fat-shaming' comes to rank with racial and gender discrimination.

None of these technical or sociological matters mattered to Amy, however. What mattered to her was the suffering she felt. She reached for the tissue box, wiped her tears, and kept the box by her side.

"In high school, I studied. Period. I hit the books. My parents—they're good people, OK? They're good people—Now they're both throwing their hands in the air. They expect me to be perfect. They *always* expect me to be perfect. Fucking *perfect!*"

She said it with the same acid tone she used with the word, 'fat.' You could almost hear her through the outer door.

"Perfect? In what way?"

"In *every* fucking way!" she yelled.

She poured herself some water from a pitcher on the end table. She seemed a bit calmer.

"When did you begin to feel that you had to be perfect? You seem familiar with being in a therapist's office. You said you were in therapy earlier? Did it help?"

"Sort of. I was skinnier. Prettier... Here...."

Amy took out her phone to find an old picture of hers with a group of friends. She was not thin exactly, but she was skinnier then, and seemed obviously proud of her appearance then.

And just as obviously self-conscious and unhappy about her appearance now

"I'd love to be that girl again.... but don't know how."

Her voice had such a longing quality, I found myself moved, seeing her struggle with tears again.

"Were you diagnosed with Eating Disorder?" I asked.

"*Duh!*" she exploded. Then laughed.

I liked her—her sense of humor, her intelligence. The way she could lighten the moment even with her tears running.

"Yeah. I had tons of therapy sessions for that! I was a cutter too... oops, I mean 'self-injurious.' I guess you know what that means."

I nodded.

"I had a food diary that I kept during high school. I religiously entered what I ate. My goal was to consume 100 calories max each day every day."

"If you reached *that* goal, you'd be dead."

"Ha! I *did* reach that goal. I not only lived on that, I looked great. I ate three or four grapes a day, plus chewing gum and water. Period. Every day. For months!"

"Really?" I reacted with a surprised look, certain she was exaggerating.

She began to open her mouth but stopped. "Well... OK, no. No, not every day. Sometimes I binge ate."

She closed her eyes.

"Tacos!"

She all but groaned.

"But I'd purge the whole thing up as soon as I finished them.

"I was in a lot of athletic activities early on. Dad

was a great golfer, and he would take me and my sister with him to the driving range all the time. I played Lacrosse in middle school and I was an amazing swimmer. Part of the swim team since 5th grade. We won the State championship in high school.

She seemingly enjoyed narrating her enriched extra-curricular life. There was a proud look in her eyes, and she kept smiling. I wasn't sure whether I should try to bring her thoughts back to the pre-senting issues, or let her keep going with her self-praise. There was no question but that she had self-esteem issues.

I looked at the time. No, we needed to focus.

"The championship! That's incredible, Amy. You must be so proud. May I ask you a question? It sounds like you were involved in quite a lot of physical activities. That must have required proper nourishment. How did your eating disorder affect that? For instance, how did you feel after purging food?"

"*Great!* Light and relieved. No guilt. No food to pack on my body. Doc," she said. She added, pas-sionately, "Being a size zero at sixteen? That gets you all the attention you'll ever need in class! I was *popular* then."

Her disposition changed completely, all at once. She sank back into the couch, and grabbed the tis-sue box and broke violently into tears.

"I am so sorry!"

She cleared her nose and grabbed more tissues.

"And now?" I asked. "Where are we now?

"I can't concentrate on my studies! They call me

a fat ugly bitch. A *fat ugly bitch!* "

"My sorority sisters are evil. I go on crash diets. I haven't had any food for days! Then I binge eat like a pig. Anything I can lay hands on—a tub of ice cream, peanut butter sandwiches, sodas, cake. You name it! I work out. I sweat out five hundred calories at the gym all the time. But... nothing works. *Nothing works!*

"I want to look normal. I want to look like *them*... the beautiful girls in their high heels and fancy clothes. Boys are crazy about them. No one is crazy about me. No one likes to be around me. I'm so fucking ugly. So fucking *lonely*... "

She began sobbing again.

"Are you still cutting yourself?"

"Last time I cut myself was two weeks ago. But it's no big deal."

She pulled up the sleeve of her sweatshirt and showed me her wrist. There were marks of razor cuts. Superficial cuts.

"It's not that bad now. I used to be obsessed with cutting in high school, it was such a cool trend, everyone was doing it. One of the girls on my swim team almost died as she cut too close to her vein and was bleeding all over. Her parents sent her to Residential"!

She frowned and looked down.

"I was inpatient during my junior year of high school. They put me up at this loony place where all the kids were doped up like zombies. It was too scary for me."

I wanted to explore that painful experience and her related emotions further. I approached the matter carefully.

"It must have been hard for you... "

"It was worse than a prison there, Doc We were marched to the cafeteria with a bunch of aides who kept a close watch on us while we picked out food trays and ate. The girls were sneaky, though." She laughed. "They would stick the entire hamburger by the back of the dining table or under their seats. Some would shove them into their bras. The idiot aides never noticed a thing,"

She wanted to keep going but looked at her watch.

"*Oops,* it's almost time, gotta run!"

She gathered all her stuff, her book bag, her purse and her jacket, and sat there in silence for a minute. There was resignation in her puffy red face and tear-swollen eyes.

"I need to get better, Doc. I *have* to. I can't go on dealing with shrinks all my life. I don't want to be in any more hospitals. You know. You know where I'm coming from."

She became quiet, as if going back in time, reliving the inpatient experience. I did know. It is not a good experience. I decided not to go any further into it. At the moment.

"Okay, Amy, here's what we need to do in the next few weeks. I want you to complete a few assessments related to your thought patterns regarding eating habits and body image".

She nodded.

"And you need to promise me to attend your sessions on a *regular basis.* Together we are going to set up some goals for you to work on that will get you closer to being a better you. The person you want to be. Okay?"

She nodded morosely and rose with a sense of resignation. She had walked in all frantic and hyper. Suddenly she looked years older, tired and emotionally exhausted.

I found the assessments she needed to fill out, gave it to her, smiled and assured her that improvement was possible. I wished her a good week.

What is a 'presenting problem'?

For medical professionals, a patient's presenting problem is often something very clearly defined. It's a loss or limitation of physical function. If you can't breathe, or digest, or walk, or see, you have a physiological problem that medical practitioners can locate and address quickly and directly, if not always successfully.

Clinicians in the mental health arena, by contrast, have a much wider and more ambiguous task. They deal not so much with dysfunction as with dissatisfaction. Many of my clients function quite well indeed. Most are high achievers. They often excel in salary, position and job performance. Yet there remain areas of their life that fill them with intense misery; severe emotional and behavioral challenges that poison and threaten to destroy what seems on the surface to be the image of success.

Nor is it emotional suffering alone that challenges them. Most laypeople understand what a physical illness is, and have a rough sense of mental illness, but find the concept of *behavioral* illness harder to grasp. Yet problems like Internet or porn addiction, binge eating, gambling, obsessive cleanliness or constant lateness, reckless spending, constant spousal bickering and argument, aren't physical ailments. They aren't even (exclusively) emotional problems, really.

The problems lie in what the person *does,* and the gap between that and what they want to do or can do, given their patterns of behavior, their life history and circumstances, and their current social situation.

As a result, we sometimes have to face not just a physical or emotional complaint but an entire jumble of life problems and have to unravel them before we can even begin to facilitate a positive change. Because it's only when a problem is clarified that the therapist can help the client move towards the solution.

There was no better illustration than Amy.

At the time of her initial consultation with me, Amy was 5 feet 10 inches tall and weighed 310 pounds.

Amy was sent to me not by her father but referred by her psychiatrist. Not yet twenty, her record showed that she was already suffering from an entire range of subjective complaints—chronic anxiety, inability to focus, depression, lack of sleep, poor concentration, and more, not to mention other psychosomatic complaints such as, migraine and high blood pressure.

I began to review her medical record. Were her psychological problems purely overt, or did they mask some further underlying medical disorder or disorders?

I found no evidence for that, but there *was* evidence of something unfortunate that I came across again and again—overmedication. Her psychiatrist had placed her on a regimen that saturated her system with drugs.

It was a big-ticket prescription drug cocktail for bipolar depression, anxiety and sleep, there were additional pills (stimulants) to help her concentrate and focus, other pills designed to correct her blood pressure, and migraine. All this on top of over-the-counter diet pills that she bought impulsively whenever an effective enough advertisement caught her eye. It seemed almost as though half the pills were there to counteract the negative side effects of all the other pills.

The battery of 'cures' she was taking for the disease *was* the disease! Or at least a major component.

I advised her to stop taking most of them, and consult with her primary care physician for physiological conditions such as her heart health and obesity.

I expected resistance. Amy's face was a picture of relief.

Her clarity of mind, the improvement in the way she felt, even her high blood pressure, improved almost at once, and significantly.

But, though clearing away the underbrush of possible medical issues and of unnecessary over-medication helped immensely, a physical problem remained. One with many social and psychological dimensions.

Amy was heavy. Overweight. As she put it herself, over and over and over, Amy was "fucking fat"!

Not grotesquely obese. Not even, in my opinion, unattractively so. She dressed well, smiled often, and had a kind open face over which a bright intelligent expression played.

But by the supermodel norms of most fashion magazines, she *was*... fat. And she took that physical fact and turned it into the foundation of an entire range of destructive extrapolations. She felt, for instance, that, socially and in terms of romantic relationships, her weight was the kiss of death; and her life story provided a good deal of evidence for her opinion.

Later in our regular sessions I learned that Amy was a military brat, the oldest with a younger sibling who was seven years apart. Her US Army father was frequently stationed in various locales, moving with what seemed like arbitrary unpredictability. Her parents seemed loving enough, but Amy made literally no friends as a child and was a bit too old to connect with her younger sister, Sarah.

No sooner would a friendship begin that her family would be posted to another locale. Her parents observed that she was lonely and out of place, but the way they addressed the problem didn't help. Her mother would try to compensate by flooding her with sweets and treats, while her father, distant and judgmental, felt she should be "a little trooper" and "deal with it." He regarded her, she felt, as a disappointment.

Whether it was an observation or a prophecy, her body grew chunkier and heavier as she grew older. There were no apparent traumas behind it, but somewhere around third grade she developed a sense of oddness and humiliation all centered around her weight.

She became the "fat girl" in the class. Children ostracized her on the playground. "We can't have that Fatty on the team, she'll slow us down." Boys would insult her and call her ugly. "Hey, Fat Stuff!" they would call out. "Skip the ice cream!"

The tall slim popular girls associated only with other tall slim popular girls, and boys she liked avoided her.

If she approached *them?* They laughed in her face and insulted her and walked away.

The low opinion others had of her soon internalized into a low self- opinion and a crippled self-image. She had no friends in elementary school and was not comfortable sharing her sadness and pain with her parents. Shame and self-contempt left her utterly miserable, so miserable that eventually even her parents took notice.

With an extremely judgmental peer group and a constant series of moves, Amy nonetheless managed to find one "true friend" who was always with her and always ready to comfort her no matter where the family transferred.

Her love for and obsession with food!

She started eating a dozen pack of chocolate chip cookies at a time. Hoarded candies, cookies, bread and other unhealthy food in her closet, under bed and would sneak in ice cream tubs late at night. Food was her friend with no judgement or mockery. She felt safe in this company and indeed satiated!

By the time she hit puberty, she had reached one hundred and eighty pounds. Her pediatrician suggested balanced diet and therapy. But parents were too busy moving again and changing towns.

By age fourteen, her mom learned that Amy had been cutting herself. They sought help. Her parents took her to the local hospital where they found more fresh wounds and cuts across her wrists. They went through her room and found notes and sketches suggesting suicide—scribbles of hanged figures in skirts, and girl stick figures with cartoon frowns and tears on their faces and pistols at their temples. In her closet and drawers there were stacks of stale and rotting food.

Amy was at that tender age when girls are self-conscious of nearly everything, and when appearance matters most. Weight loss had come to obsess her. It had reached to the point where her health began to visibly suffer quite aside from the self-cutting.

To her parents' credit, they took immediate steps beyond just seeing a doctor. Her father, to her surprise, put an end to his wayfaring and settled down to one post near a small town in California so Amy could have a stable school environment and finally make friends. Informing the local hospital, physicians there referred the family to an eating disorder specialist at a clinic not far from her new home for long-term therapy.

It worked. To a degree. Having a stable environment in high school helped Amy with noticeable progress. She maintained a food diary, never missed her appointments with the specialist and a recommended dietician. Her parents paid extra attention to her—especially during meals. She joined the local health club and played tennis and golf during summer break.

She even lost weight.

But not for long. She lost weight when she starved, and her weight exploded when she started eating again. At the extreme point of her starvation, she would take photos of herself that she cherished. Amy, thin at last! But it never lasted. Starvation wasn't sustainable. And while her efforts did show some physical improvement overall, the mental issues associated with it—her *attitudes* toward her weight, and the self-image she constructed upon those attitudes—fluctuated wildly.

The therapeutic help Amy was receiving did indeed manage to help her shed several pounds during High School, and that left her much happier, allowing her to focus on her studies and even take part in parties and school events and other extracurricular activities. She was back on track.

But being *slimmer* was not being slim. A smirk

from thinner fashionable girls in cliques, rejections from boys when her weight returned, would sink her into intense depressions. On one occasion she overheard boys 'ranking' the girls in the class for attractiveness. One boy to whom she was very attracted laughed when her name was mentioned. "*That* fat pig?" He placed her at rock bottom.

Amy left the classroom and went home to her room where she lay on the bed in tears. There she stared at the scars on her wrists.

*How nice to put an end to all this,* she would think. *No more doctors, no more therapy, no more people judging me and snickering, no more binges and purges and gorging and guilt and uncontrollable food.*

*I can be free of this misery. My parents can be free from this misery. They're good people. They don't deserve to be stuck with a fat ugly problem child like me. All it takes is a knife... a nice sharp kitchen knife...*

"And what happened, Amy?" I said.

"I went downstairs to the kitchen to get a knife. I figured I would take a bath later. Open my veins. Unfortunately Mom was in the kitchen at the time. I couldn't get to the knives. And soon it was time for dinner."

She smiled crookedly. "Besides. It was apple pie with butter pecan ice cream. My favorite! *So* fattening!"

She laughed. But not that day. That day she had dinner with her parents, and as she ate, Amy's despair, her suicidal thoughts, passed away. Or at least lessened.

She ate, excused herself, and went to her room, took out her sketchbook, and sketched knives and skeletons and gravestones.

With Eating Disorder in adolescents, I like to look at the family dynamics. Amy's family were a mixed case. Her mother had over-indulged her as a child. Her father had been often absent yet critical and brusque.

I could see how environmental factors had mattered over-eating and comfort fostered by the mother, added to over-eating to compensate for felt rejection by the father, all contributed to the condition.

Her father was clearly the major factor in her life: he was extremely organized and clearly had high expectations for his daughter. Amy was expected to clean her room and do all the age-appropriate chores since early elementary school.

All the decisions and choices regarding her 'well-being' were made for her by her father and she never questioned it. There was pressure to be a high achiever, but most of all there was *order*, prescribed by her father, to which she was expected to conform. Her early home life functioned much like her father's professional life: on the military model.

Amy worshipped her father and trusted her to make choices for her. He made the choices for the family as a whole and for her mother as well, and the mother was a model for Amy too—a model of submission.

I found myself wondering whether Amy's weight problem might be something more—a form of rebellion, an assertion of freedom in an unfree situation. In many respects she had grown up controlled, and her weight, being out of control, was perhaps a psychic space all to herself, a protest.

But I pulled back from that easy interpretation. A therapist is not there to theorize but to help. Was it helpful to carry around a dozen or even a hundred unnecessary pounds as a protest, even a just protest? There are better and far less self-destructive ways to assert one's freedom. And was her home life really the cause of her unhappiness?

The exact cause of eating disorder is unknown. There are numerous risk factors that increase the chance of developing the disorder—risk factors including parents passing on their own poor eating behaviors, physical and sexual abuse, being bullied and teased, which she certainly had been at school, even genetics.

But none of these seemed to be the case, and while the family showed some early dysfunction, those factors seemed to have been cleared away. There was no more rootless drifting or fatherly absences. Her parents were stable in their marriage with no apparent financial issues or power dynamics. There was apparent love and respect in the family. Clearly, they were ready to make significant changes to help their daughter.

I asked to speak to the parents.

They flew into Chicago to see Amy and joined in for a session, and they were just as Amy now described them: full of love for each other and for their children. Overall, a very balanced picture of the family! Maybe Amy's picture of her early family had been exaggerated—or maybe those years had simply been the chaos some families pass through before they settle down.

Here was an area where therapists must tread carefully. A good therapist accepts what the client brings to her. If Amy had *felt* very controlled during her childhood, then that was how she felt. It was not my job to dispute her felt experience but to work with it—to work *within* it, for a therapist can only meet a client on *their* ground. If a client feels that the therapist has no understanding of their problem as *they* see the problem, nothing can be done.

Those days could very well have left their mark and fostered eating and emotional habits that persisted even after the initial situation establishing them had passed. But they had passed, and Amy did not feel that way about her family now. That was a fact of her experience also. What then accounted for her persistent weight issue? Was it simply that—a persistence of mental and behavioral patterns from childhood?

Somewhere, I came to think, Amy had come to idolize and inherit the perfection and orderliness her father had ordained and began projecting it on her body: to be perfect was to be thin. Her schoolmates reinforced this principle, constantly and cruelly.

*Thin* was celebrated, *thin* was attractive, *thin* was *in*. But getting there was not for everyone, not for the *weak*: it demanded tremendous control and self-discipline.

Amy was *not* thin, however, and therefore she was imperfect, flawed, lacking in self-discipline, a *bad daughter*, a *failure as a person*. Her obesity was not just an appearance she presented to the world but an internal self-definition, and an extremely negative self-image at that. It was not just that she was 'fat' but that the fat testified to an inner debasement sparking nothing less than a self-hatred that was dark in the extreme.

In her *opinion*. Was that opinion true, was it a thoughtfully and mindfully considered opinion, was it perhaps—a mistake? Amy was heavy, yes, but hardly ugly. The question was, what did 'ugly' mean for Amy? Partly it meant constant self-denigration. Partly it meant anticipated social rejection—by schoolmates, by the opposite sex, by other people in general. There she was not mistaken: she had seen the pretty girls with the pretty smiles get all the attention many times, and she had even learned a few lessons from that observation.

But there were things beside weight that people found attractive, and Amy had and cultivated those things. Amy could *charm*, and she often spoke with a wit and intelligence and optimism that made her company a pleasure. But to be attractive in her own way was a hard constant uphill struggle, and how she envied those whose thin appearance allowed it to come naturally and easily.

As her High School years concluded, Amy had turned a corner. Her family had finally settled, and Amy's therapy during her high school years had borne fruit: she'd made progress with her treatments, and the cognitive-behavioral exercises for a positive self-image her specialist had recommended were working, and exercise and a healthy diet were working too. Amy began to change her outlook towards her body and mind. She focused upon her academic performance and graduated high school with Honors, and recognition by her State. Her parents were proud of her.

She entered a prestigious university intending to major in computer science, expecting nothing but good things to follow.

Finally, *finally,* she was 'in control.

Disaster followed.

Moving far away from her hometown and adjusting to a big city lifestyle was not easy for Amy. But she felt that she needed to assert her identity, to demonstrate to her parents and herself that she could live her life the way she chose without her parents constantly hovering over her. Her parents were concerned about the distant move, but eventually reconciled to her choice. After all, she no longer cut herself; she had overcome the demon of eating disorder; she was disciplined and orderly now.

And she would not be alone. A sorority had accepted her. There would be friends and a community there to support her. At least so they assumed.

That was not the case. Her college sorority was a daily chaos of drama and drinking and catty competition, heavily seasoned with drugs and parties and boys. Amy was soon swept up in the tide of sexual promiscuity and excessive drinking that was the sorority norm, and her disciplined approach to living, like her disciplined approach to eating and exercise, soon collapsed. Her out-of-control behavior led to multiple visits to the local Emergency Room and inpatient stays.

She tried to, and did, keep most of what was happening from her parents. It didn't keep Amy from sinking deeper into depression, confusion, misery and loneliness. Her grades started falling and her weight began to rise significantly. She was put on academic probation. At times, she felt like dropping out and going home... but the imagined expression on her parents' faces stopped her.

There was one light in the darkness, or so she thought. She had met a boy who told her that he loved her. His name was Rick. They had met at a frat party, and, unlike most of the boys she met at such parties, he'd asked for her number and wanted to see her again. She said she'd like that too.

Rick was no longer a student at the university. He'd dropped out, he said, and was working at a factory to make some spending money before going on to complete his education. They started dating regularly. She began thinking of the two of them as a couple. One day, maybe, as a married couple. She began dropping hints to that effect, and to spend evenings and weekends overnight at his tiny city apartment.

The college sophomore had turned a major corner in her life. She was in love. She picked up her grades and started working hard. She grew less interested in college parties and dress-up socials. Her obsession with a perfect body began to fade. She encouraged Rick to get back in school too. She could see a better future for both of them. It almost seemed like she was playing house with Rick, confident that they'd make a great couple.

It didn't turn out that way.

After announcing to her parents that she had a boyfriend, she was fated to yet another trauma, Rick got evicted from his apartment for not keeping up with the rent payment. He also showed up drunk one day for work, and lost his job for that and for being generally incompetent.

He left Amy a note. The hell with it, it said. He was going back home to Nebraska. By himself.

Amy was devastated. Devastated and all alone. She decided to drop a semester and go home too. She couldn't take it anymore either.

Her parents were fully supportive and worked with her during this time. They took her places, overseas trips and family gatherings. She took up a job in her hometown working at an animal shelter. She loved it.

With constant support from her family, and because she genuinely did want a good education, she returned to college. She was not obsessing over her weight to the extent she always did; she had become resigned to her weight. Somewhat. She continued through summer and decided to work on all the courses she missed. She dropped out of her sorority and shared a small apartment with another student, Emma.

Locking herself away in her dorm was not a wise move, though. Poring all the time over books and studies, sitting hour after hour in a chair in fron of a computer screen, became a grind. She slipped slowly into binge TV watching, and marijuana abuse, and sheer motionless torpor.

Needless to say, she overate. That went without saying.

There were days, sometimes weeks, when she struggled to get up and failed, when she would not open the shades even to see the daylight. Old demons came back, and she started cutting again. There was a soothing comfort to watching blood ooze out of her wrists, down along her fingertips

She'd pull herself together, briefly, go without food for days, then binge and binge further. Her weight mushroomed.

Her roommate, Emma was concerned but helpless. Amy didn't want her to contact her family or college regarding her condition, and Emma complied—till, one day after class, Emma returned back to the dorm to find Amy unconscious on the floor, overdosed on prescription medication.

Emma called 911.

Another long journey of inpatient treatment in the behavioral health unit of the local hospital began. Her parents were on her side this time—supporting her, not condemning her. She promised to get back on track and to follow through with treatment.

The doctors now diagnosed Amy with Bipolar Disorder with Borderline Personality traits, and she was placed under the care of a psychiatrist for regular medication management.

The management method seemed to consist of showering her with an avalanche of drugs. Amy had gone that route before. Depressed, passive, obese, falling into thoughts of suicide, she looked for another option.

The hospital gave her several outpatient referrals for continued therapy.

The name 'Rashmi' caught her eye.

She called my office.

Reviewing Amy's interview, her questionnaire responses, her medical history, her life history, I could see certain things right away. She was not psychotic, nor out of control. Suicidal fantasies and wrist-slashing raise alarm among all competent therapists, but I could see too that none of her attempts had been serious enough to even distantly risk actual loss of life. They merited close attention, to be sure. But a gain in stability from a reduction of overmedication might be a better path to that.

I suggested she stop her meds entirely, and she

gratefully complied. Her mood lifted and her school and job performance improved significantly almost overnight.

I did *not* address her weight issue, not directly, and not at first. A therapist is not a dietician or a nutritionist or a personal gym trainer. She had had all of those, and once upon a time they had helped her to be slimmer. I knew that she knew how to take the same road and lose weight again.

My concern as a cognitive-behavioral clinician was with her thoughts and her behaviors. Were they supporting her and helping her reach her goals, or were they crippling and frustrating her? Her behaviors seemed to be positive enough. She was going to school again, avoiding cliques and parties that were awash in drugs. She was going to a gym. What about her thoughts, the cues and rationales for these behaviors?

There I could help by giving her what she seemed never to have had: simple, unconditional, empathic acceptance. Someone who would listen to her and not condemn her. Her parents had never given her that. They had always set a standard for her to reach, which she had never quite reached. She had never even given *herself* that.

She condemned herself even more harshly than her parents. She was always imperfect, always failing. I pointed out her many personal and academic successes: they were not enough. Every success was minor and soon forgotten, every mistake and failure inflated to self-lacerating intensity and relived mentally over and over again. Relived, but not mindfully explored.

In one of our regular therapy sessions later on, she drifted back towards self-degradation.

"I'm such a disappointment to my parents, to my little sister"! I can never, *never,* get back their love and respect."

"That's true," I said. "You can't get it back because you already have it, and you always will. Your parents *love* you, Amy. You know they do. Your sister loves you. And they're proud of you, too. Why wouldn't they be? You were an award-winning High School student. You're a student at a top-tier university. You're here because of a scholarship you *earned.* You're here, *period.* You *didn't* throw your life away. You've *survived.* Don't you think you deserve some respect for that?"

Does it sound like I was disputing her statements? No. I was asking her to *examine* them. Don't imagine that the job of a cognitive-behavioral therapist consists of contradicting whatever a client says, or giving groundless pep talks. The task is to get the client to thoughtfully examine what they say to themselves; to have them *look* at what they say to themselves objectively, sometimes for the very first time, and unearth the unnoticed underlying assumptions.

"I'm fat. I'm *ugly,*" Amy would say.

"You are a little heavier than some women of your height, yes, and also a great deal lighter than other young women your age and height. As for being ugly, I don't think you are, and the boys that have asked you out for dates don't think you are. Are you really saying, Amy," I would ask, "that fat people are worthless? Amy, do you know anyone that's overweight?"

"Yes."

"Do you *hate* them? Do you think their lives have *no value*? When you see someone who's a little heavy, do you run away from them down the street shrieking?"

She laughed—always a good sign. "No."

"Do you have friends who are overweight?"

"Yes."

"Are they *hideous?* Do they *revolt* you? Are they *monstrous?*"

She laughed again. "Well—no."

"Do you enjoy their company? Do you like them?"

"Well—sure. Yeah. Yes, I do."

"Statistics say that over two-thirds of Americans are overweight or obese. Two-thirds! Do you think that *none* of them ever go on a date, or get married? Do you think that *not one* of them have any worth as a human being?"

"I think all of them have worth as a human being."

"*Including you?*"

I could see the impact of that question on Amy. There generally comes a point in my talks with clients when they stop talking. When they look within, or outward at their behaviors, and start understanding. When they understand things differently. More supportively. More charitably. When the conversations blossom into insight.

This happened quite early and quite often with Amy. Reducing the number and amounts of meds were a good start. Simply listening to her pour out her thoughts and feelings, without judging or condemning, was a good next step. Helping her to examine those thoughts and feelings lifted our sessions to an entirely higher level.

Did she really *have* to be perfect? To reach every one of her parents' goals for her without even forming her own? To be paper-thin?

The 'trick' to holding an effective therapeutic communication isn't a matter of inserting one's own ideas into a talk in order to change minds. It's a matter of helping a person with maladaptive thoughts to see those thoughts clearly for the first time.

Could Amy's value as a human being be *reduced* to the numbers on her bathroom scale? No. It was as simple as that.

In her own words, Amy was setting out on a path to recovery: "My relationship with food," she wrote to me in an email, "was based upon my relationship with my body, how I perceived it and how I accepted it. I never realized I was a control freak... a perfectionist. No, that's not right. I never wanted 'perfection': I was only punishing myself for not being born perfect from the start. I was using perfection. Using it to justify beating myself up. I'm learning the hard way that not being perfect and indeed a size zero is okay and not a failure on my part.

"I'm proud of being honest about my feelings now. I don't need to be critical of others or myself. My friends feel comfortable around me—the *real* me. They're even beginning to be more authentic themselves. I'm their model, Rashmi! If I can recover from my inner demons, they can too."

And she *did* recover. It took a while for Amy to straighten out her thinking to her own satisfaction. It took a while for her behaviors to reflect those thoughts. But slowly, like a broken bone healing, Amy's new and consciously ways of constructive thinking and acting bore fruit.

Amy has since done very well indeed. She went on to graduate with honors. She did marry. She's settled down happily. She has a child now, and a successful career—all the things that are really not so hard to achieve once we manage to get out of our own way.

She did *not* lose weight—at least, not to 'size zero.' (A good deal of excess weight is lost naturally when you have children, a husband, a job, and visit the gym three times a week.)

But she did something more important: she learned to regard herself as intrinsically valuable whatever her weight—to *accept* herself.

Everyone who wants to be better than they are—and we all want to be better than we are in some respect—has a choice. They can realize that even in our imperfect, as-yet-unimproved state, we have intrinsic worth; that though we choose to strive for the better, what we have and are still has value and is still essentially good. Or they can decide that only our ideal has goodness—that if we have not yet reached that ideal, we are crippled and ugly and evil.

This second viewpoint is completely false:

every life and every situation has value. Yet so many of us, so often, tell ourselves that because we don't have everything we want, because we aren't everything we want to be, who we are and what we do have has no value. And so we fall into the void of self-hatred.

This can lead to great pain and deep personal tragedy. Yet, fundamentally, it is nothing more than a *mistake*. A mistake that sober, systematic, attentive cognitive reflection can clear up.

I can't leave the story of Amy without adding a personal note. One of the most shocking, and moving, moments of the treatment occurred one day when, impulsively, she took a group of notebooks out of her bag and pushed them into my hands. She walked out and left, not wanting to sit and watch my expression as I looked through them. I soon understood why. The books were a number of diaries that she'd kept starting at the age of fourteen when her obsession with weight loss was at its most extreme.

I turned the pages and was horrified.

There were cut-outs after magazine cut-outs of skeletal supermodels, girls with flat, exposed abdomen, thin arms and legs, hollow cheeks and bony pelvises. There were pictures of Amy—with X's crossing out her 'fat' face, and obscenities and self-abusive language scrawled over her own features. Quotes such as "I pray to be a skeleton goddess," "Happy girls don't eat!," "Food is sinful!" jutted against cruel scribbled caricatures of her own 'fat face.'

She jotted down her daily eating record: a thirty-calorie diet of grapes, chewing gum and water each day, for day after day after day. There was no positive outcome and her weight remained the same. She felt ugly and undeserving of her parents' love. After all she wasn't the "perfect daughter," not with that ugly, heavy body, and a weak will unable to attain the same. She *failed* herself and she'd *failed them!* She was *garbage, trash, worthless.*

In the depths of many such sad moments, she would cut herself "to punish" her body. Her thoughts were distorted to the point that she wrote, *happily*, that "starving and self-mutilating will eventually kill me' and I won't have to go through this ordeal no more."

She was suffering the amazing delusion that she would find happiness through self-mutilation, through running away from her own flesh and more deeply from her emotions.

We all know in the abstract that a person who feels unattractive is probably unhappy. But going through Amy's diaries showed me the full and chronic *depth* of pain and misery that many such people go through. I knew that Amy's condition was painful; not till I opened her diaries did I have a sense of how *much* pain she felt, and very how long she had carried the burden of that pain.

I respected her all the more, knowing how much courage she had shown, bearing so much unhappiness, and yet moving forward regardless. And—grasping the magnitude of her pain—I was determined all the more to help her.

But the same time I wanted to protest. As a clinician, I am a humanist, and as a humanist I am necessarily a feminist. Women still bear a burden of discrimination that is real, and unjust. Still, reading Amy's notebooks, I felt a kind of anger that women should allow themselves to fall into such self-torture over something as shallow as appearance.

Why should women have to bear the *burden* of beauty? Why should *we ourselves* place so much importance on slimness, on youth, on a pretty face? Why should physical attractiveness matter so much more for women than men? There is nothing wrong in wanting to be attractive, but to go through such devastating suffering as Amy's notebooks record when one is not, is a tragic error.

When I closed the notebooks, I had to make an effort to retain my objectivity. The job of a good therapist is not to *dwell* on a problem; it is to solve the problem, or at least to point out a direction that the client can follow that may help solve that problem, or reduce the suffering that accompanies it. Simply contemplating the depth of suffering some clients experience doesn't help the client, and can swallow up the therapist as well. "Gaze not too long into the abyss," wrote Nietzsche, "lest the abyss gaze into thee."

Amy's notebooks showed me the full and awful dimensions of pain and suffering which some women experience over their appearance. I'm content with my own appearance, and tend to regard dwelling on one's looks as just a little silly. But looking into the abyss of Amy's writings, the abyss looked back into me, and I was shaken.

I don't think I have ever *under*estimated a client's suffering since, or done more to honor it with a full measure of empathy and respect.

CHAPTER SIX

# THE LAKE

Clients who come to cognitive-behavioral therapy are encouraged to focus on their successes—
on the things they do well, the things that bring
them satisfaction. Not all therapies share that perspective. Some favor dwelling upon a particular
problem until (it is hoped) the unconscious yields
up some hidden clue that will illuminate the issue;
illuminate it so much so that, ideally, the problem
simply vanishes away.

Studies suggest that that doesn't happen very
often, and it's not how CBT approaches personal
problems. CBT encourages the client to dwell on
those moments of their life in which they function
well—the areas that bring joy, heighten meaning.
These elements tend to support mental health.
Case history after case history in CBT suggests that
dwelling on the good and the positive, understanding why the good and the positive *work*, generates
more of the good and the positive.

In my experience, the same thing applies to the
cognitive-behavioral therapist: often the cases

that have been the most successful are the ones that most deepen the therapist's understanding of his or her craft, even as they lift up the client.

This was especially the case with a client I will call Grace. Few cases began more darkly. Or ended more happily.

Grace entered my office with considerable *panache*. She was a very well-dressed woman, obviously affluent, trim, polished and educated. She appeared to be in her fifties and must have been rather beautiful when younger. She was still attractive, and carried herself with a calm, cool, self-contained air, an air of being in command. (I later learned she had been a high-level hospital administrator.)

The only thing that concerned me about that first business-like impression was a certain flatness in her expression—a lack of affect. Other than that, though, she seemed like a woman of note who was not in any obvious need of therapy at all.

I was wrong. After introducing herself, she explained that she had been recommended to me by her psychiatrist who was the latest in a long, *long* string of psychiatrists who had been treating her. Literally for decades.

"Treating you how, Grace? Medically?"

"Yes."

"For what?"

"Depression, principally," she said. "Intense, severe, non-stop depression." "I feel like I'm covered under a heavy wet blanket all the time. I can't breathe, I feel like I'm being suffocated"

"How long have you been feeling this way?"

"Fifty-six years."

I paused. I was tempted to point out that no one can be depressed non-stop for over a half-century. Human emotions fluctuate, feelings rise and fall, come and go. She had to have experienced at least *one* happy day, one spontaneous chuckle.

But one is not there to argue with clients. One is there to understand and help them.

"You say you've been treated medically. Have you been in therapy before?"

"I've been in therapy for over twenty years, Doctor Pandey. I've been in PTSD group therapy for sexual abuse for nearly ten years." A streak of anger marred her face. "I'm *sick* of therapy. Sick of it. I have therapy exhaustion."

"And none of it has helped?"

"Therapy doesn't change things, Doctor. It can't change the past. Talking, drugs—they can't change what's happened to you."

I leaned back.

"Tell me more."

Grace went on to tell the story of her life, and it was a painful story. She explained that she had been abused by her parents in the most demeaning and vicious ways since infancy. They were a prominent and wealthy Connecticut couple that had made a name for themselves in finance and local politics and society, and, to hear Grace tell it, she and her siblings were raised as decorations appropriate to the parents' smug social station. But they received no love or affection or notice.

At least that was the case with her siblings. They were lucky enough to be ignored. Grace, however, had been singled out from childhood for extreme humiliation, cruelty, and outright sexual abuse. She told me that, at age five, her parents would take their prominent friends up to her room and force Grace to undress for them. She stopped there, her previously cool face now contorted, now livid with emotion. A specific emotion: hatred.

My heart went out to her.

But, for a therapist, sympathy isn't enough. Some degree of sympathy is an absolute necessity for establishing a connection and understanding. The goal of therapy, however, isn't simply to share a client's feelings, but to help repair them. We may share in their tears, but our larger task is to dry them. To do so I needed to learn more, and so I encouraged her to continue.

At some point the parents grew bored with tormenting her, she said. They sent her away to a private boarding school in California at age fourteen. She ran away and arrived in Los Angeles at age seventeen, where she fell into nightmare experiences of poverty and living on the margins. She experimented with narcotics, committed petty theft, slept with various men. Was drugged and date raped and in due course one of them left her pregnant.

She was pressured to abort. She refused. And so, at rock bottom with a child on the way and with nowhere else to turn, she called home. Much as she still despised them, she asked her parents to take her back. They might not do so out of love, but they might to avoid any scandal smearing their reputation. Grace threatened to make that scandal very public if they did nothing.

They found her a room, and saw that she got through the pregnancy comfortably. And quietly.

From that point, almost like a miracle, Grace's life began to turn entirely around. She gave birth to her child, found a job at a local hospital, settled into a new apartment, and began dating when she met a young aspiring surgeon. They fell in love, he adored her child, and they soon married. The new family moved to Illinois, where she completed her education. She had another child, then another, and together the couple began to rise swiftly in both their professional careers and in the local community.

"Pardon me," I said, "but—that's wonderful. You say you've been depressed literally all your life, but it sounds during those years you were... well, happy."

She shrugged. "They were better years than the ones that came before. That's true." She stared directly at me. "But it's like icing on a rotten cake crawling with spiders. You can dress it up, cover it over. You can't cover up the rot underneath. I tried pushing all that out of my mind. Pretending it never happened. It didn't work."

"So you decided to go into treatment?"

"My son died. My first son."

Her mouth twisted.

"Following in my footsteps. Like mother, like son..."

Grace had determined, she said, that her children would *not* have the childhood that she had had, and she and her husband pampered and spoiled their children in every way they could. The children were not spoiled at all, they all came out of it wonderfully, she claimed, and she loved them all.

But when her first-born son was seventeen he left to go to college, and without warning bolted and ran off "to see the world!" He ended up in New York City, where he began taking hard drugs, and became addicted. Unlike his mother, he did not recover, and died of an overdose without ever reaching eighteen. His body was identified, and shipped home. Grace was crushed.

But she survived. She was used to weathering storms, she told me. Besides, she had other children to safeguard, a husband who genuinely loved her, and important and humane work in health care. Like all lives, hers was a combination of darkness and light, and there was sufficient light to give meaning to her days. She told herself that she had every reason to live, and she did live.

But the darkness, an emotional darkness that had surrounded her from childhood because of her parents, intensified; she blamed them for her wretchedly miserable childhood, her wretchedly miserable adolescence, her wretchedly miserable years of poverty, and now its wretchedly miserable consequence—a lost, dead child.

Her parents. She *loathed* them, and loathed them with a hatred that was incandescent. Most of her life she had been able to push the dark material in her mind aside, she said, almost as though it were not there. But after the death of her son, those childhood memories exploded in frequency and intensity. She assured me that not an hour would pass without her returning in memory to some horrible incident that would instantly spark *spasms* of barely contained hatred for her parents. Her composed outer life was a facade: its burning core was incessant passionate fury directed at the monsters who had given her birth.

Therapists often witness a kind of transformation in their clients. They enter the office wearing their everyday facade, but the longer they go on, the more the mask slips. That was how it was with Grace. The cool sophisticated exterior vanished, revealing deep, at moments almost savage, pain and instability.

"And how long have these memories been disturbing you like this?"

"'*Disturbing*' me? *Twenty years!* All my *life!*"

I needed to consider her case. I gave her my client questionnaire, and said we would have to talk further. I thanked her for being so honest with me, and added that I looked forward to our next session. She looked surprised.

Her questionnaire arrived by email prior to our next meeting, and it confirmed at least one suspicion. She was—like so many others—on an entire battery of drugs. Anti-depressants, anti-psychotics, appetite suppressants, sleep aids everything. It was the usual story. She took sleeping pills to get to sleep at night, and Adderall to help her get through her hectic day at work, drugs to keep off weight and drugs to stifle anxiety. None were medically necessary. They were 'mood drugs,' drugs for the mind, not the body. The high number of these medications was bad enough. Their interactions in her specific case, unknown. The prescriptions she was taking were a prescription for disaster.

In our next session I said to her that—with the help and agreement of her psychiatrist—our first therapeutic goal should be to taper off her medications. *All* her medications.

Her jaw dropped.

"Are you *joking?*" she said.

She was shocked, and resistant. "I—I wouldn't be able to function."

"We're not going cold turkey. We're only considering a reduction in the dosage and number of prescriptions for now. But eventually, yes; if possible, our goal should be to get rid of all of them."

She said nothing, and looked lost. For a moment I feared she would get up and run out of the office in panic, clutching bottles of Prozac and Adderall near to her beating heart.

I spoke to her gently.

"Just stop taking few drugs for now—the most toxic ones. See what happens. See how that makes you feel. I have no doubt whatsoever that you'll feel better and that we'll see an improvement in your mood and behavior. *If* that happens, then we can reduce the amount you take of some of the remaining ones. Does that sound reasonable? Don't worry. We'll take it slowly and safely."

Reluctantly, she agreed. And things worked out exactly as predicted. As she and her psychiatrist slowly weaned her off her meds, Grace showed marked improvements almost at once. The roller coaster of her inner experience slowed down: the hours of slack emotionless torpor punctuated by manic bursts of hatred abated.

Soon she went off all her meds except the lowest dose of anti-depressant, and the cool exterior she presented when we first met faded. As I suspected, she had not been cold and distant by nature—only drugged into numbness. The livid outbursts, like protests against her narcotic state, moderated too. Her face and body language now became more relaxed and humane.

From body, to mind. As our talks continued, I wrote in my case notes that the problem seemed to be a simple one: obsessive thinking. The cruelty she'd suffered at the hands of her parents was despicable and criminal. But what was done was done. Her parents had passed away. She was right: you couldn't change the past.

However, changing the past was not the problem. The problem was that Grace never stopped revisiting the past. She constantly brought the past into the present by thinking about it. It was a kind of 'evil mindfulness,' an intense conscious regular focus of the attention, but on material that was painful and self-destructive and nothing else.

The intensity itself was a gift—if she could place it on more proper, supportive objects. The focus simply needed to be placed elsewhere.

Standard CBT approaches were the clear first step: homework assignments in which she recorded positive moments and times of the day untouched by her negative memories; therapeutic discussions that helped her realize the uselessness and self-destructive nature of dwelling on what could not be changed; becoming mindfully aware of her thoughts, so as to guard her from being mindlessly swept away by them; focus on what strengthened her rather than depleted her. We simply needed to redirect her attention.

But then the story took an unexpected turn.

When discussing client problems, CBT therapists like to look for exceptions to those problems. If a couple seems to be constantly arguing, for instance, we will ask if there are any times when they are *not* arguing. There are almost always such times. What characterizes the times when the problem is *not* happening, we ask? How can we encourage more such exceptions? How can we make those times last longer?

Grace would say to me time and again that she was *always* depressed and always *had* been depressed. I asked her if she was less depressed now that she had stopped taking multiple anti-psychotics. She laughed, and admitted she was.

I then asked Grace if there were any specific times when she was not depressed. When she thought of her husband, was she depressed? No, she said, smiling. He was wonderful and she loved him very much.

Did the thought of her soon-to-arrive grandchild depress her? Not at all. She beamed at the thought.

And what about her parents, I said? Surely there

must have been at least one or two pleasant moments...

She exploded. Never. *Never!* Ever since she began to remember the *things,* they had done to her...

"'*Began* to remember'?" I said. "What do you mean?"

Grace explained that until not very long ago she had completely forgotten the *vicious, vicious things* her parents had done to her. She'd forgotten them for years. She had always *hated* her parents, she said, but she had never realized why until she was in her forties.

Only then did the memories of those incidents begin to return to her...

Sometimes they would come to her in dreams, sometimes during the day, but in each case, they were so *vivid,* so *detailed,* so *real.*

Grace had no doubt they were real, no doubt whatsoever.

The memories *felt* so real.

The memories were so terrible to deal with...

She must have suppressed them...

I nodded. But suddenly the whole picture had changed.

Grace had given me the impression that, prior to the death of her son, she had pushed her memories of abuse aside. She had made it sound as though the memories were there, but too painful to dwell on. What she told me now was that there *were* no memories of sexual or other outrageous abuse prior to her son's death.

"I suppressed them completely," she stated. "I must have."

But did she? Had she suppressed the memories, or had she fantasized them? Was it her memories of abuse that caused her hatred of her parents, or was it her hatred of her parents that created memories to justify them? Had the traumatic death of her son been some sort of catalyst?

Grace suffered, and suffered terribly, from the presence of an absence. But were actual suppressed memories of abuse the 'absence' that so tortured her, or had the early absence of love and care from her parents led her to create false memories to justify her anger at their indifference?

Was this a case of repressed memory? Or false memory syndrome?

And did it matter?

Repressed memories—and false memories, also—are a matter of some controversy in the psychological community. The consensus nowadays in the psychological community is that our memories are in most cases reliable but never perfectly certain—not so much recorded as constructed. The mind isn't like a library of perfectly accurate tape recordings. It's more like a set of stories, stories told from a particular perspective by a novelist who goes back to touch up and revise them as time goes on. Different people remember things differently.

Studies confirm that if ten different people witness an accident, the ten stories that follow will differ too in several minor and not-so-minor details. However, all ten will agree that there *was* an accident. Memories may be individually tailored to fit, but they differ from complete fantasy.

In most cases. But not in all. In some cases, what is recalled is completely false. And when a mind is filled with significant and powerful false memories, it suggests that something is seriously wrong with that mind.

Had I been mistaken? Were Grace's 'memories' false, and masking some more serious condition? How could I be reasonably sure?

Some psychologists think it's obvious that intolerably painful memories will by definition not be tolerated. The person suffering them will blot them out. Others feel that sufficiently painful memories *can't* be forgotten. We may forget our car keys, but not a rape.

Was it reasonable to think that Grace had simply squashed all specific memories of parental abuse for over forty years? If they had occurred, it would account for the hatred she felt for her parents. If they had not, then why did she hate them so? Simply because they were cold and indifferent? The fact that these apparent memories surfaced only after the death of her runaway son was another element of the puzzle. Had that been a trigger of some sort?

I found myself facing not just a factual dilemma but an ethical one. For therapists, sanity and reality are interwoven. We try to help clients see and accept reality as it is. Therapy is not a process in which we promote whichever lie provides the client the most immediate comfort. It is not our job to build fantasy worlds for clients to inhabit, because fantasy worlds eventually fall apart, causing only harm for all concerned.

With Grace's permission, I looked further into her background. I spoke to her siblings. They agreed that their parents were distant and unkind. But certainly not abusive. There had never been any other negative reports about the parents—no police reports or arrests, no treatments for alcoholism or spousal abuse. Nor was there any evidence of a history of abuse in their parents, or in the larger family.

The more I looked, the less hard evidence I found. It *might* have been as Grace remembered it. But there was simply nothing to confirm it. Her stories were so vivid and so outrageous that it was hard to believe that there was nothing whatever to initiate them. Yet nothing whatever was all I could find.

I came to believe that her memories were in fact false; that they had never happened. Each of the few times I tried to raise that possibility with Grace, she rejected it violently. The memories were so *clear*, she said, so *vivid.* How could they not be true?

Which left me in a dilemma. Should I try to *compel* Grace to accept what *I* thought was most likely true? Or should I meet my client on *her* terms, and work with what *she* felt to be true?

Of course, the question answered itself.

What was false was not the memory, perhaps, but my dilemma. Whether the status of the memory, the solution was the same. Grace's attention needed to be directed *away* from obsessive, repetitive concentration on these painful memories. She suffered because she continually relived them. True or false was not the issue: she needed to move on.

In a comment on analyst Heinz Kohut's posthumous monograph, *How Does Analysis Cure?* authors Rowe and Isaac wrote that "only through empathy could one come to an in-depth understanding of the inner life of another person... it is only through immersion in the client's experience that the analyst can hope to gather relevant, in-depth psychological data as a true basis for clinical understanding..."

True enough. I was not there to *battle* Grace. I was there to help her cope with a crushing burden. Could I do that best by arguing with her immediate personal experience and her most intense feelings and beliefs, or by accepting them and helping her try to find the best way to deal with them?

As I thought about it, I had to shake my head and smile. I was doing what so many of my clients do: I was over-thinking a problem. True, false, what mattered, what was needed was to get Grace to focus on the many blessings with which she was surrounded. Those were undoubtedly true, undoubtedly real.

And so, we both began to walk the long and systematic road of examining and changing not her memories, but her *reactions* to those memories.

One of the joys of being a therapist—and yes, it

can be a joyful profession—is seeing someone in utter misery completely turn around and become a happy, fulfilled, positive, *sunny* personality, free of the weight of unhappiness that drives them to therapy in the first place.

When Grace first came to see me, I was dumbfounded to hear her mask of a face inform me that she'd been suffering from deep, constant, intense depression for years, for literally decades, of unrelieved misery!

And today? I honestly do not know of a happier person. She is *radiant.*

No, these changes are not miraculous. They take a while. A complete change of attitude is not something that happens overnight, and it doesn't happen through authoritarian rudeness or manipulation. At no point does the cognitive-behavioral therapist ever lecture and hector the client or say "You're wrong" or "You're stupid." The therapist accepts that, for whatever reason, the client has fallen into particular patterns of thinking and acting, and (among other assignments) simply and repeatedly asks the client whether a particular way of thinking is helpful, or a particular action is the best way of responding.

Did repeated spasms of violent hatred *help* Grace or did it *harm* her? Was dwelling on memories of brutal abuse and sexual torture making her life better or making it worse? The question answered itself. I never confronted her by saying that her memories were false. Perhaps they were! But the past was not the problem. The way she lived her life and thought and felt in the here and now was the problem—and the solution.

I remember the day when she digressed and began telling me about some awful image in her childhood—and then just stopped.

"Oh God," she sighed. "That memory is so old. So *boring*. I don't need to think about that again," she said.

She looked at me, and laughed.

"I'll just throw it in the lake!"

It became our catchphrase, our mantra.

*Throw it in the lake!*


Grace has been my client for over fifteen years, and now, when we connect, it's like being with an old friend. We've each come to know a lot about each other's lives. She likes to be *my* therapist at times, and sends me lovely thoughts and greeting cards. I honestly feel a genuine bond with her.

Over the past fifteen years, we threw a great many things in the lake. We continue to. It's made Grace a much happier person.

But what has made her a *radiant* one is that Grace has learned, not only to direct her mind away from painfully useless thoughts, but towards richer, more uplifting ones.

Now, when we talk, she tells me about her joy at her growing number of grandchildren, her retirement travels with her husband, the books she loves, the way she's redecorating her home, the active part she still plays in profession and in her community. Her life is full of enjoyment and achievement, *and she is continually aware* of those things now.

Before, she lived her life against a background of horror. Now she lives her life before a background of satisfaction and joy.

Nothing has changed except her perspective—her regular way of thinking.

But that is enough.

Grace still visits me—on Zoom, these days, since she and her husband are often visiting her grandchildren or halfway around the world. She doesn't need to, but she says her visits make her feel better.

I feel the same way.

.

# CHAPTER SEVEN

# LOVELESS

Clare is the very image of success—or at least, success as many in the American business world would define it.

Clare is rich.

Clare is at the top of her profession.

Clare is presently the highly respected manager of a highly respected hedge fund—a fund of which you may well have heard.

Clare is eagerly sought by headhunters for high lucrative corporate slots and salaries.

Clare is in high demand as a speaker and panelist at professional events and conferences.

In her late thirties, Clare is also trim, attractive, beautifully dressed, surrounded by all the prizes corporate success can bestow: elegant cars, stately homes, glorious vacations, a portfolio of profitable investments.

Fame, respect, beauty, wealth. What more could a person desire? People who see Clare whizz past in her shiny Porsche must think, 'Here's a woman who has everything she could possibly want.' A woman totally fulfilled. The last woman in the world in need of professional psychotherapy.

"Dr. Pandey?" she said when I first picked up her call, "Please. I need to talk to a therapist. Badly. *Desperately.*"

Money and the need for therapy have an interesting relationship. Poverty has its own unique constellation of psychological issues, and they are not mysterious—self-esteem issues, self-image issues, stress, frustration, limitation, anxiety, difficulty in affording adequate treatment, poor nutrition, and so on.

But few of us are as aware of the mental disorders that can accompany affluence. Suffering from affluence may sound like a paradox, even a little affected.

But while the mental stresses and perils of affluence aren't as obvious as those of poverty, they can be no less painful and destructive.

At first glance, the core problem of affluence would seem to be a problem of freedom. The very affluent can indulge themselves, and so many of them do—in corrosively destructive pastimes. The poor can't maintain $10,000 a day cocaine habits very easily. The very rich can.

The affluent can change their *external* circumstances much more easily than most. What they can't change is their *internal* situation, their *selves*; that sense of who we are and what we face and what we've done that accompanies us like a shadow. They can't change their thoughts and feelings, not without a great deal of self-examination, introspection and mindful self-reflection. In short, without a great deal of therapy.

The greater freedom that affluence brings is often balanced by a strange sort of unfreedom. Some became affluent through ferocious workaholism, tying the whole of their identity with their corporate status. Their work lives become everything, their personal lives nothing.

Often there may be social segregation. The rich do not live in the same areas as the less rich, or belong to the same clubs or schools, or eat at the same restaurants. There may be a suspicion, a fearfulness, a lack of trust, regarding others. Are their friends *really* friends, or only pretending to be because of the money?

The easy access of the affluent to toxic drugs, false relationships, and addictive indulgences can be crippling. I've seen affluence virtually destroy some of my wealthier clients, clients who I'm sure would have been happier living more modest, more moderate, lives.

Clare was one such client, who seemingly had everything.

And who felt all of it came to nothing.

I see my clients on Saturdays only once a month. Clare chose one of those Saturdays for her initial visit. She was unable to spare an hour for therapy during her fourteen-hour weekday work schedule and frequent traveling assignments.

On weekends the floor of my office is quiet. The

receptionist is usually home on weekends, and no one's present at the reception desk to greet people. So that Saturday I came down personally to the reception area to welcome Clare.

There she was, gleaming and unmistakable! A tall, beautiful woman with superb bearing standing there in her weekend-best *haute couture* summer attire.

As she watched me approach her, she coolly raised a eyebrow. I thought of Mr. Spock.

"Doctor Pandey?" she said, with a superior look that implied I might be the concierge. I was almost tempted to laugh.

"Yes, I'm Doctor Pandey," I said. "And you must be Clare."

"Normally the first time I see a therapist, they're sitting behind their desks under their diplomas in front of a wall of bookshelves. It's a marketing ploy, of course. A power game thing. Something to establish status. Authority. I do it myself."

This time I did laugh. "Not all therapists are that calculating. Have you seen enough of us to really generalize?"

"Dozens," she said, not smiling, "upon dozens." But then, suddenly, she did smile, a bright, genuine smile, and offered me her hand.

I found myself thinking that here might be a classic example of projection. Clare was assigning to me the desire to make an impression; but her own presentation of self was obviously crafted for effect. Sometimes what clients try to look like can tell you more about the person than the person can themselves.

Clare? I found her self-presentation rather appealing. She seemed strong, competent, brave; there was a crispness and confidence about her. She seemed the sort of person likely to get straight to the point, and not play games.

Yet she had come to see a licensed psychotherapist. Urgently, she said. Apparently she had seen many. One right after the other.

Why?

People imagine that providing therapy means working with dysfunctional people—that every client is some sort of twitching wreck, if not outright mad. Not so. The truth is, many of my clients are highly successful, highly effective, highly respected individuals. They do quite well in in most aspects of their life. Professionally, they can be spectacularly competent.

But there is *one* area of their life, or one or more private areas, which nags at them with repeated anguish and pain. Sometimes they protect it as though it were a secret; sometimes it is so hidden that even they don't know it themselves till some undeniable mishap. Sometimes they don't know reason or the cause. But they know the effect: a persistent sadness, distance or despair.

Clare was that sort of mystery. As I walked her to the elevators, she commented on the building like a master realtor itemizing its commercial virtues to potential millionaire buyers. As we rose up to my office, we made small talk—the state of the economy, international affairs, the trends of the day. As she entered, she looked around, complimented my office décor, and chose to sit by the large picture window overlooking the busy stretch of Magnificent Mile, the upscale section of Chicago's Michigan Avenue. She gazed at its major department stores and international brand name designers and boutiques, and her gaze was a seal of proud approval.

Then she turned to me.

"What am I doing here, Doctor?"

"You tell me, Clare," I said

"I can't. I'm not sure what I'm looking for, Doctor."

"That's probably why you haven't found it."

"You think you can help me find it?"

"I believe I can help you clarify your thoughts and your feelings about what's bothering you. That may bring you closer to whatever it is you're looking for."

She didn't sit down. She paced.

"I'm... unhappy. Very unhappy. I want to stop being unhappy. Silly, don't you think? Isn't that a silly goal?"

"Being happy all the time, every moment of the day? That's silly, yes, in the sense of being an unrealistic goal. But being happier than you currently are? Being more satisfied with yourself and your life? That's always possible."

She nodded. She paced.

"Every life has good things in it and things that are not so good," I continued. "If you can direct your attention and spend more time considering and cultivating the good things, and dwell less on the bad things, you're likely to enjoy life more. Sometimes you can even take steps to improve the bad things. That isn't at all unrealistic. It's always possible to do better, to feel better, to be better."

"So my goal should be to redirect my attention?" I smiled.

"Instant diagnoses are what you find in fortune cookies, not therapy. In most cases my client and I set goals in later sessions. It can take many sessions to bring real clarity to a person's situation. Or, sometimes, just a few. Making changes in that situation? Sometimes it involves examining your thoughts and beliefs, sometimes it involves changing certain behaviors, sometimes it involves making a change in your relationships or environment. It depends."

She nodded. "That's reasonable. And true. I recently moved here from LA, and I had a great therapist there. We had some profound talks together. She helped me with several issues. Tremendously."

We talked briefly about her background and personal history, and she responded in a rehearsed manner, like most clients with previous therapy experience do. Yet she was confident and comfortable. When she alluded to her unnamed personal problems, there was none of the more usual tears or sobbing: she spoke with perfect pitch.

What was it that bothering her, I wondered? She seemed more than equal to any task, including that of facing the demons of the self

Then she looked at me, switching gears instantly with intense eye contact.

"My current boyfriend just broke up with me,"

she stated. It was a cold sentence devoid of emotion. "I met him at my girlfriend's wedding."

I nodded. "Was it a long relationship?"

She shrugged. "A few months. As usual."

She sighed.

"Shane and I were made for each other. He was the most handsome man I ever dated. Perfect in every way. We met every single weekend, even though he lives in New York. It was a match made in heaven."

She looked down at her nails. She frowned. One was chipped.

"We broke up last week. He came down for a visit and took me to 'Maple & Ash' for dinner."

She fidgeted. "He dumped me. He *dumped* me. He said he wasn't ready for a serious relationship at this point in his life... he felt like I was pressing him into... a commitment. Like... I would ask him, 'When are we going to call each other boyfriend and girlfriend, Shane?' *That's* supposed to be a *commitment?*"

The pacing got faster and faster.

"Why? *Why?*" The cool articulation was now a whine on the edge of tears. "Why do I *do* this all the time? Why do I get so desperate?... *What's wrong with me, Doctor?*"

One moment, Margaret Thatcher.

The next moment, a jilted high school girl.

Of such transitions is the life of a therapist filled.

What was wrong with Clare wasn't immediately obvious, and it wasn't 'wrong' in any moral or irreparable sense. Like most personal problems, it revealed itself over several subsequent sessions: Clare always liked to have things her way. My rational-behavior colleague, Dr. Albert Ellis once called this, inelegantly, 'musterbation.' Things *must* go the way I want, people *must* act the way I want them to, everyone *must* meet the standard I set—even me!

Essentially, it's a need for control. Obsessive control. And the problem is that it assumes that situations are constantly spinning out of control, forever unstable and uncertain. That's why control is so necessary, and constant. Clare acted with confidence in every area of her life, and radiated self-esteem. But as I got to know her better, the insecurity accompanying her self-esteem soon showed itself.

"What if he doesn't like me?"

"What if I'm just unattractive?"

"What if I'm getting old?"

"What if I'm just not the 'relationship type'"?

The unrealistic downs were followed by equally unrealistic ups.

"I'm the *best, Doctor!* The best in *everything I do!* I'm *rich.* I'm *hot.* I'm...

"*I, I, I, I, I,*" I said. "Are you saying that you're perfect in every way, Clare? That everyone *has* to be attracted to you? That they *have* to see you as you would like to be seen? That they *have* to do what you want them to do?"

"No, of course not. That's..."

"Silly?"

True enough, there *was* a sense of perfection in everything she did, and she *did* seem to do almost everything well. Clare was nothing but pleasant and full of life. She was helping, warm, supportive to her friends and family, and a diligent worker. You never felt any pressure! And yet there was something asphyxiating about her self-advertised 'perfection'; something asphyxiating even to her. You felt that you were watching an actress giving a brilliant performance, not that you were connecting to another human being.

Clare was new to Chicago, but she thrived in company and in no time established a large group of like-minded local friends, fans and admirers around her. Soon she had everything she wanted in the new city but... her shallow connections to many masked the reality of a deep connection to no one. What she wanted most was what she did not have: intimacy. Not someone to perform before, but someone before whom she did not have to perform, only be. She wanted not to feel so utterly alone.

Clare sometimes made me think of another of my clients, Maya. On the surface, Maya was the opposite of Clare. Chaotic, unstructured, forever drifting from relationship to relationship, Maya never seemed able to sustain a lasting, loving one. She would pass from minor life crisis to minor life crisis, all against a backdrop of chronic loneliness.

Clare's life could not be more different: Clare hummed with optimism, competence and efficiency. She set her sights on goals, and she achieved them, economically, directly and with speed and rigor.

Yet in the end she and Maya both seemed to always be ending up in the same place: isolated and alone. Why?

A therapist is there to help her clients, not speculate; and I like to think that I do help them. But it may be closer to the truth to say that I help them to help themselves.

Our minds, like our bodies, have a tendency to heal naturally. The job of the therapist is to assist that natural process—to help the client better understand the problems that nag at them, to provide a space of acceptance where the client can (sometimes for the first time) breath free, to suggest approaches to solutions or remedies that the client may not see at all.

The welfare of the client is the heart of the therapeutic relationship. What I've called 'structured empathy' is structured around the person most in need of it, not the therapist who applies it.

But the exact nature of that need, like the way to resolve it, is not always immediately apparent. The problem a client presents is sometimes—not always—a cluster of problems, or a symptom of some other, deeper problem.

Clare's problem was in one sense very simple and practical: whenever she went out with someone, three or four dates would happen, and then the person would break the relationship off or stop taking her calls.

"Rashmi—what am I doing *wrong?*"

Yes, I know this sounds a bit silly, like the opening of an American television commercial where only the right toothpaste, cream or deodorant is needed to transform the buyer's love life. But it wasn't a shallow matter to Clare, who would spend evening after evening by herself, a success in every way but emotionally.

In Cognitive-Behavior Therapy we teach the client to observe the (often dysfunctional) things they are saying to themselves.

But we also get them to watch and describe their behavior, and we look at the environment in which that behavior takes place. All these things are interrelated, so as therapists, we encourage the client to change one or more of those elements, even if only in small ways at first. As they do, the whole configuration shifts.

But one needs a point of entry. And my first talks with Clare seemed to point to no obviously psychological sources of her problems cause. She didn't think of herself as unpleasant or unintelligent or unattractive. Nor was she! The talks she reported with her companions over dinner seemed lively and entertaining. They took place in excellent restaurants and establishments. Her dates were often with peers in the business world or well-salaried professionals who moved in roughly the same circles and 'spoke the same language.' Yet invariably the connection would quickly peter out. What was the problem?

I began looking deeper and opened a conversation into her history.

Like Maya, Clare had been born in relative poverty to a German father and a British Commonwealth mother. She was the only girl in a family that included three older brothers. The brothers received the lion's share of her parents' attention, especially from her father.

The neglected Clare did not stand out in childhood, or in middle school, or in college. Like Maya again, her college years were a blur of experimentation with drugs and sex. But she did not stand out in that regard, and seemed to be going nowhere, other than passing into the long unfocused drift that marked lives such as Maya's.

And then—everything changed. Slowly at first, then radically, her entire life turned around. Turned around, and took off like a rocket.

Why? What made the difference?

From what she told me, very little—but more than enough. The key was leaving college and having to find a job. There, at first, she drifted too. Some of her friends had submitted their applications to a large financial corporation, and had gotten accepted. Clare followed the herd, not really interested and not really expecting much, aiming only to pay her bills.

But something about her job in that large corporation took root. She was given tasks to do and targets to reach and step-by-step training drilled her in the ways to reach them.

Something about her new life, about the *structure* it gave to her daily activities, stuck.

Her work life became a series of projects one after the other. The way to complete those projects was clear, and the rewards for doing so were large. Over time she became focused and efficient and became accustomed to demanding efficiency from others. She commanded staff and her team obeyed.

The better they all did, the higher she rose. The path up the corporate ladder was quick and clear and inspired her to rise further, and the ever-ascending roles she filled were each time more notable and profitable.

But those were only results. The company had given her something much more important than a set of business objectives to complete. It had given her a methodology. A *way* to achieve goals. The clarity of that new approach became addictive, and soon Clare expanded it to other areas of her life—to how she spent her private time, to how she conceived of her values, and to how she managed her relationships.

Clare had become a True Believer—in systematically controlling her environment.

As she rose higher and higher in the company, as her salary and savings grew (she had little time left to spend her earnings), by her late thirties she found herself independently wealthy. But with no wish to retire. She had gotten so used to filling her days and nights with work that the notion of leaving the company was unthinkable.

She was supremely accomplished at her job. The problem was that *how* she accomplished it was the same approach she took to living her personal life. Like a discrete series of projects directed from above. By Clare.

It wasn't hard to find what drove Clare's isolation. It was the same addiction to *control* I've seen in other high-profile business clients. When Clare was with someone in a personal situation, she did not 'go with the flow' or 'live in the moment.' She did not relax or take things as they came. She did not stop to enjoy things. She did not *stop* or *enjoy* at all—she planned, pushed, and achieved.

If Clare felt an urge for company, she would never just go to a party, or sit down for a coffee with a stranger, or pick up someone at a bar. Every meeting had to have a *point,* an *objective.* Relationships? Relationships were not casual. They were not about affection, or fun. They were a contract. The objects of her affection had to meet strict criteria beforehand—*high* criteria.

At one point Clare joined an elite dating site, a high-profile site where you were "selected" based on your professional profile. Cost of entry: $10,000. Clare's profile was so stellar that she was selected often. But each date so arranged had to be planned beforehand—by Clare. Each would keep to a strict schedule—dictated by Clare. Clare would decide where they ate, and what they ate. Clare would decide where they went, what they saw, what they did.

She treated her few close friends the same way. If they got together to have lunch, it was at a place Clare wanted to go. If the group decided to go to a spot not of Clare's choosing, Clare didn't go. Time with Clare was not so much spent as executed. Clare found that efficient. It was, when that time was spent on a business project. Off the clock, those along for the ride found it coercive and awkward, and in the end tiresome.

For Clare, the work/life balance had been totally swallowed up by work, but in a strange way—not literally, but operationally. Clare viewed her business life as the planning and successful execution of a series of organized tasks. That mindset had become a thing of habit, and it had bled over into her personal life. Her friendships, her romantic relationships, were a series of projects now too. Her 'free time' was not free: it was a set of steps to be executed in the proper order at the prearranged time.

But life is not a diagram or a set of algorithms. Human beings are not players in an orchestra, all of whom are seated in pre-assigned seats playing the same notes in a finished, unchangeable score. It's more like jazz, where common melodies are shared, but each player improvises, and at times several players improvise together. Sometimes the result is a surprise of great beauty, and sometimes it falls apart into noise. Nonetheless we take the risk, because that risk brings with it freedom and creativity and self-expression. And often beautiful music.

Clare did not want to take that risk. Or rather, she was not aware that taking a risk was an option, because she'd fallen into the habit of handling her life with only one strategy: planned oversight. Which is why newfound friends and romantic interests soon finding her grating. Whose idea of a good time and a happy relationship is always being told what to do?

There is a saying: "To a hammer, every problem looks like a nail." It might perhaps be more accurate to say that a hammer treats every problem as a nail. Like OCD, the hammer repeats and repeats its single action over and over.

That isn't always a bad thing. In some cases, a hammer does what it needs to do. But repetition for its own sake becomes a dead end.

That was the problem with Clare. Clare had become a hammer. Her personal life, like her professional life, was a series of pre-ordained steps. A date and a staffing survey involved the same series of actions: research, candidate interviews, selection, training, and termination if performance criteria were not met. It was not what most people search for when they look for love.

I sensed that there were deeper emotional drivers too. Beneath the mask of control there is nearly always a very different face: the face of insecurity and fear. The controlling person is driven by an unacknowledged but corrosive sense that what they have is unsure and fragile, that at any moment it can be ripped away.

Clare's childhood had been like that. Her parents' affection could be and was withheld. At college, girlfriends transferred, boyfriends graduated, drugs wore off. Corporate life became to Clare an exception to that rule—an oasis of certainty and order, a step-by-step strategy detailing where to go and what to do. A strategy marked by quick reinforcement and rich rewards. That she should extend it to other areas of her life was no surprise. It worked, and she had come to trust it completely.

Until it stopped working.

I was there the day that it did stop working—the day Clare was let go. Laid off from her hard-earned, high-earning, seemingly impregnable lofty position.

Clare was shocked—but far from devastated: business involved realism, and Clare knew that downsizing and headhunting and moves from one company to the next were a part of business life.

She was nonetheless shaken, and I could see growing signs of depression infecting her. It was hard for her to see the crisis for what it was—an opportunity to grow.

As with her relationships, she now needed to 'think differently,' re-invent herself, find a new approach to dealing with a new situation. And that she did, wonderfully melding her active goal-oriented way of life with new and creative ways of addressing her new challenge.

She sketched out new businesses that she could lead, new startups that she could begin. She explored other companies and knew what steps to take to find a new position.

Soon a new position appeared. She expressed an interest. She was interviewed and hired.

It took six months for Clare to fully re-integrate into the corporate fold, and while those six months were harrowing, they were also creative. The loss of her job severed her relationships with her colleagues, and with that her social life plummeted—reduced itself, in fact, to little more than visits to her therapist: me.

But that also was an opening she used to best advantage: as she began to see me less as a sounding board and a consultant, and more as a genuinely empathic friend, the more she began to open up. Our sessions, and her self-understanding, deepened.

There *are* therapists—bad ones—who actively impose their views and values on clients. Often, they're completely wrapped up in some particular school of therapy, intransigent devotees of Reich or Klein or Skinner. They know the client's problem and the answer to the problem before even meeting them!

That's not my approach. I have several very affluent clients, and while some would call them workaholics or obsessive in pursuing their career goals, I see no fault in that provided they genuinely *love* their work and their jobs. Their goals *should* inspire and energize them! It isn't my task to *dismantle* the psychological engine that's lifted them to eminence, to tamper with the drive that's brought them genuine pride and life satisfaction. Rather it's to help the client adjust its workings, to fine-tune the accompanying thoughts and behaviors just a little, but also just enough to address felt pains and unnecessary unhappiness that sometime go with a life of achievement.

So, with Clare. In many ways her approach to life was a good and productive one. It had taken her from a life she felt was going nowhere to a life in which she took a good deal of justifiable pride. It just wasn't a good approach on a romantic level.

The problem, I came to see, was to free her from the prison of one strategy, and one strategy applied to an inappropriate area. And here I had a wonderful ally and resource: Clare herself.

One of the challenges therapists face is what are

called 'homework assignments.' For the client to step away from the painful consequences of what they're doing, they need to do things differently. Simple and obvious, yes?

But getting clients to understand what they need to do, and getting them to actually do it, are two different things.

One of the way behaviorists address the problem is through a process called *shaping.* If an assignment is too hard for the client to execute, we craft one that is easier; and if that one is too hard, then we come up with one that is still easier.

If a client is afraid of asking someone out on a date, for instance, we may have him (or her) ask a librarian or a bank clerk in person for information. If that is too hard, we may ask them to rehearse their request out loud during a therapeutic session, or to do so to a photograph. We try to get them to *approach* the thought and/or behavior, starting in the least disturbing fashion, and slowly coming closer and closer, till eventually we reach their goal.

But however reasonably we may explain it, or how safe and simple we try to make the assignments, some clients just don't do them.

Not Clare. From a therapist's perspective, she was a dream come true. She approached therapeutic progress—sanity itself—as just another project, clearly defined, measurable, and to be followed up on time with a concise report. If I gave her a behavioral assignment, she would carry it out, quickly, crisply, efficiently, and state the results at the next session.

For instance? Dating. Clare had no problem *getting* dates—she was too attractive to have any problems there. But having gotten an invitation, I would ask her to make a point of asking her dates where *they* would like to go, what *they* would like to do, how *they* felt about things. I asked her to let *them* pick a convenient time for them and have her meet it.

She was puzzled. Why would she do something someone *else* wants to do? But I could absolutely count on her to complete her homework assignment, and she did, to the letter.

She was almost shocked to find that the follow-up requests for dates not only did not peter out but became a steady stream! She learned something even more important: sometimes the dates she left unplanned were delightful. Sometimes the restaurant the companion chose was novel and interesting. Sometimes the food her date selected was something she's never had, and turned out to be delicious. Sometimes she'd ask her date to talk about themselves, not about her current business challenge, and Clare would get an answer that was touching, or funny, or unexpectedly useful, or profound. It was almost literally eye-opening, because she was learning to direct the glance of her attention to so many things surrounding her that she had never bothered to see.

Watching Clare *blossom* as a person—there is really no other word, for she unfolded like the leaves of a rose—I thought, not for the first time, of the power and the limitations of therapy. It really is one of the most effectively structured ways ever developed to change human thought and behavior. Clear, direct, focused, and rational. Follow the steps, arrive at the results.

It was uniquely suited to a crisp logical mind like Clare's, given by nature and habit to planning and execution. And yet there was something mysterious too that almost slyly existed past the edges of the system—call it the existential, the spiritual, or (as I prefer) the empathic. It was indefinable and impossible to measure, and yet it was always there.

Contrary to the old saying, therapy can not only bring the horse to water, it *can* make it drink. But the moment when the taste of that cool water *registers* on the awareness, *presents* itself with all the vividness of the real—that moment is magical. Following a rote pre-planned series of steps really can't capture it, and yet one has to take those steps even to be in its vicinity.

Which brings up the most important such step: what we call *mindfulness*.

Many of us live our lives on automatic. Not merely in the sense of going to the same daily job, following the same regular routines, but in the far more deadening sense of *thinking* and *feeling* in the same tired rigid patterns. We eat fast food without paying attention to it or noticing the taste. We watch the sun rise and set without noticing or caring or any sense of wonder. We move uninvolved through much of our day as though through a waking dream.

But it's not a dream. And we *can* wake up. We can shake ourselves awake. It's an experience we've all had—waking up blurry and half-asleep, and then, after a cool splash of water over our faces and a hot cup of coffee, going out to meet the world sharp and alert. That sense of greater awareness, and self-awareness, is always available to us. We can learn to pull ourselves up to full attention.

This was the great advance, the great new landscape, that Clare began to discover.

To Clare's credit, she was not interested in having a long-term relationship purely because she was expected to, or in order to look at the same face year after year. Rather, she had a felt sense that a life lived alone, even a productive life, loveless and unloved, was only a shadow. She wanted more than company: she wanted wholeness. Connection. She wanted to live a fully human life.

The assignments I gave helped her connect to others, and to better maintain that connection, but it was only a beginning. I could *instruct* her to reinforce her dates with a kind word, a feigned interest, a relinquishment of control, and she would comply.

But I could not get her to genuinely *care* about the person she was with until she could see that person, experience that person, as an individual in and of themselves, and not as object needed to complete a therapeutic homework assignment. She needed the *substance* of a happy relationship, not a mere performance of a happy relationship.

Mindfulness was the key. She began to learn more and more to give her attention to the other person. To see them as beings valuable and interesting and even beautiful. She began to no longer instrumentalize others, regarding them as means to an end. She was learning to appreciate them for their own sake, learning to give her even her daily experiences that same disinterested attention that, paradoxically, confers affection and appreciation on them for what may be the first time.

Has that provided Clare with paradise? The classic American husband-wife-and-two-kids-in-the-suburbs scenario? Not as yet. Nor does Clare especially crave such an outcome any longer. That's the thing about mindfulness: not only do you become more aware of your thoughts and actions, you become more aware of your values.

Clare keeps in touch with me to this day. She calls me 'her person.' But she doesn't feel she *has* to see a therapist, or *has* to have a long-term relationship that *has* to be a perfect match in every way. Her romantic relationships are no longer a task: they are what they should be: a pleasure, and a source of meaning.

Clare is, as I said at the beginning of this chapter, is a success. But her success is no longer restricted only to net worth or other externals. Her work in the world, and her success in that world, still gratifies her, and rightly so. But what she's begun taking away from therapy is an additional gratitude and enjoyment of her *entire* world and the things and people in it.

Not surprisingly, her new emotional world outside work, and the people in it, appear to be responding in kind.

Is it fair to say that paying greater and deeper attention to one's world fosters greater and

deeper affection for it? That it really is only another way of learning to love? There are mystics
who might say so. As a therapist I can only say that
the ability to love and the likelihood of being loved
seem to go hand in hand.

# CHAPTER EIGHT

# SUCCESS STORY

I'll call this next client 'George.' I call him 'George' because he looks so much like the actor, George Clooney.

Like George Clooney, my George was blessed with very good looks and piercing blue eyes. In fact, he was blessed from birth in almost every way possible.

He came from a very prominent and well-respected Midwest family. His father was an established attorney with his own law firm. His mother worked in real estate. They were not grotesquely wealthy, but they were wealthy enough to ensure that their children could choose lives that developed in any direction that they wanted.

George suffered no childhood abuse, no childhood trauma. He was raised in an idyllic country home vivid with emerald forestry and azure lakes and passing horses. He attended Episcopalian services with his family every Sunday. His siblings looked up to him; his parents doted on him.

George seemed bright and brave and well-liked from the moment he could first toddle, and when he was old enough, he went to the best private school in his State. There he excelled both on the soccer field and at his studies. He left high school as class President and class valedictorian and passed directly to a prestigious Northeastern Ivy League University.

His high school sweetheart Dana soon joined him at the same university. Their mutual goal was to marry after college and enjoy a perfect home in the suburbs with a white picket fence and three beautiful children. And, in the course of time, they did build that home and that white picket fence and have those three beautiful children.

There was nothing surprising about that. George was smart. Competent. He got things done. He was going places. High places. Entering college, he had a simple goal: he wanted to be really, really rich, and spectacularly successful.

For him that meant entering the world of finance. So, for his academic concentration, he focused on banking and finance capital and the creation of financial instruments for international trading and investing. It was all very esoteric, at least as he later explained it to me, but it was also one of the fastest possible routes to accumulating a personal fortune. His parents had favored him with a small allowance and a not-so-small trust fund. But George wanted to become rich on his own. And fast.

He became rich. And fast. Once out of college, he

joined the Chicago Mercantile Exchange and then moved to a private equity firm specializing in banking credit swaps and loan margin optimalization, an area of financial investment that was a mystery to most (myself included). Mysterious or not, George attracted notice there fast, and rose at meteoric speed to become one of the superstars of the Exchange. It was a life of swift and stellar accomplishment, and success in every way that mattered, at least to George.

Till all of it crashed. Disastrously, and almost overnight. And cost him everything.

The culprit was not accident, not chance. All the blame fell to George. So he would tell me, bitterly, over and over and over.

To be specific, the cause was his susceptibility to drugs and alcohol. His parents were teetotalers, and for George college was all about study, not partying. Friends in his financial classes at college assured him, however, that not all drugs were self-indulgent 'party drugs.' There were stimulants that could help you focus and concentrate better.

George tried some. His eyes were opened. They *did* help George focus! It helped him concentrate better on his nonstop quest to be the greatest financial genius of our time. He kept up the habit even after graduating. He kept increasing the number of pills and the amount of the dosages. Moreover, in his new position among the elite financial circles and clients with which he began to regularly engage, he noticed cocaine usage was becoming popular, even a pass into certain very rich circles where cocaine use was actually rather common.

George wanted to be part of those circles. He began using cocaine too. Occasionally. After all, the investment numbers he worked with soared and plunged and fluctuated. It was stressful. At times even frightening. Cocaine consoled him, gave him a new and different high, an intoxicating sense of invulnerability. Stress simply dissolved. He felt drunk with confidence.

True, that sometimes led to overconfidence, which led to poorer work results, which led to anxiety. But when that happened, there were always more stimulants. Except that it was hard to sleep after too many stimulants. He found a doctor who gave him a prescription for sleep medication. Only then he would wake up groggy. He then asked his doctor to prescribe medications to help him wake up. When those didn't work quickly enough, he took more stimulants to kick it up further. And some bourbon to wash it down. And if that failed to clear his mind? Well, there was always more cocaine.

He asked his doctor for more medication. The doctor refused and warned him about the dangers of abusing medication. The doctor wanted to do a blood test, and said he intended to cut back slightly on the medication he'd been prescribing. George exploded and stalked out.

But he soon calmed down. After all, you didn't need a prescription for cocaine or alcohol.

The drugs and drinking affected his work, of course, leading to pressure and anxiety. For relief from the pressure and the anxiety, he took more drugs and drank more. The more he took, the worst his performance became. Things began spiraling farther and farther out of control. He began making mistakes. He cut corners, he lost accounts, he began to cost the company money. A good deal of money.

"What I *should* have done," he began (a phrase that I would hear from George over time and again) was..."

"George, you can't change the past," I would, reply, time and again. "What should you do *now?* What's the very best thing you can do *right now?*"

But that was not what I said that first time. That first time I wanted to hear his story.

"What I *should* have done," he said that first time, "is taken a leave of absence, gotten off the worst of the drugs, and gotten counseling immediately. Or, I don't know, maybe I should just have resigned. Quit everything, found a hotel room, gone completely cold turkey."

"But you did not."

"No," he said, "I should have. I could have gotten another position elsewhere. Eventually."

"What happened instead?"

He looked like a prisoner in a police interrogation room. He put his face in his hands. He took his hands away, and looked up with a tragic expression.

"I screwed up. Badly. I signed off on some international funding exchange. The numbers were all wrong, the wrong instruments were traded. It was a disaster. The company's clients lost millions. Millions. What was worse, from my perspective, was that I got a massive commission from the exchange before it all fell apart. It was alleged that I did it deliberately to pocket the money and blow it on drugs.

"And, you know? Maybe I *was* doing it for that. I don't *think* I was," he told me, "but I'm not sure. Most days by then I wasn't conscious enough to be sure.

"Anyway. I ended up in court facing criminal charges. The clients who'd lost their money went on to sue the company too. I returned the commission, but I still had to pay fines, and my attorneys. It took nearly all I had to stay out of jail. But then the *company* lost the suit. That did it. I was done. I was fired, of course. But more importantly my professional reputation was ruined. My life was over."

"If your life were over, George, you wouldn't be here. Life goes on."

"Yes it does," he said. Coldly.

He wrung his hands. He straightened.

"I stopped being invited to the kinds of parties where the cocaine was free. I began drinking cheaper and cheaper brands of alcohol and got into harder street drugs. Crack. Meth."

He shook his head. "I thought I'd hit bottom." He smiled crookedly. "Doctor, I didn't know what bottom was."

"Did your family offer to help?"

"In the beginning. My parents let me stay with them. Till I got back on my feet. After I started doing meth, they stopped. I can't blame them. I began stealing from them. They offered to give me money if I'd seek professional help. *'Help'!"* he said, cynically. "I didn't want *'help,'* I wanted *drugs.* I wanted something to *drink.* When they cut off the allowance they were giving me, I blew up. Screamed at them, smashed up the house. They were terrified. They put a restraining order on me. My wife already had. I'd been screaming all sorts of filth at her, night after night, in front of the kids while the court cases were going on. The kids cringed in the corner, holding each other and whimpering."

His voice choked as he mentioned his children.

"She tried to calm me down," he continued. "It didn't work. I beat her up in front of them and then I went through her purse for money and took her car keys so I could go out and score more drugs. I was completely out of control, and crashed the car into another driver. We both ended up in the hospital and I found myself back in court.

"Let's make the long story short, Doctor. I lost everything. Lost the house. Lost my wife and kids. She just packed them up and left. Vanished. I can't blame her. I don't know where she is now. I don't want her to know. She's better off if I don't know. My kids are safer if I don't know. My parents don't speak to me anymore. They froze my bank accounts, the trust, everything. My brother and sister won't pick up the phone. Why should they? They know it's that *bum,* that *parasite*, George, trying to hit them up for some money for a drink or a hit. And they're right!"

"You're still engaging in substance abuse, then."

George laughed. "*Yes*, Doctor. I *am. Hell* yes. As

my medical report states."

"If your accounts are frozen, how do you manage to pay for them? Do you have a part-time job?"

He shrugged.

"I stand on the corner of intersections and hold a sign that says, 'Disabled Veteran' or 'Blind' or some such garbage and hold out my hand. Sometimes people put a dollar in it."

"Where do you live?"

"In a halfway house"

I laced my fingers together and frowned.

Let me tell you one of the dirty little secrets of the therapy profession. We therapists don't take everyone. People who watch too much TV that touches on psychotherapy imagine that the professional therapist takes on only the most spectacularly warped of patients—serial killers, multiple-personalities, violent maniacs.

Nothing could be further from the truth. Therapy attracts the therapist because it places the therapist in a situation where he or she has a high probability of success. Problems like multiple drug addictions, severe brain damage, neurological genetic disorders, are hard *physiological* problems. They don't respond well to therapeutic conversations or insights.

A therapist's field of operations involves not the body but ideas, behavior, language, self-talk. Therapists know that people experience grief or anger, depression or loneliness, anxiety or obsession, not because of unchanging objective physical facts but because of our *interpretation* of those facts; because of the words that we say to ourselves over and over that cement that interpretation into the only one we can see.

That is why "The Talking Cure," as Freud called it, cures. In the course of several conversational exchanges, as we examine our thoughts and feelings and problems, we gradually develop newer and truer and more beneficial understandings of those problems.

Just as we change physically as we grow older, so we change psychologically: the simple fact of ever-accumulating experience allows us to revisit things in our life from a different perspective.

Addiction, however, is not a problem of interpretation, and the royal road to its resolution is not conversation. Addiction is a physical ailment. It modifies brain function, neural pathways, dopamine levels, response times, hormonal responses—an entire range of physiological states.

Yes, there is a psychological *component* to those states, but to try to alter a physiologically injured body by sheer brute force of mind is to court failure. The addict needs to get over his or her physical addiction before the mental healing of therapy can take place.

This most therapists know, and many know it through bitter personal experience. Normal therapeutic approaches simply won't work. Moreover, the addicted client is the client most likely to explode into violent verbal and even physical abuse. They are dangerous to take on, and painful to work with, because the result is almost always failure. The addict client will swear time and again that they are off drugs for good, but sad experience has shown therapists that they will backslide down to rock bottom again. Fast. The therapist becomes like Sisyphus, pushing a heavy rock up a steep hill, only to see it roll back down again, over and over.

So, my first inclination was not to take George at all. After all, he had come to me by complete accident. George had indeed more or less destroyed his former life, but there were two aspects of it that he had not destroyed. One was the comprehensive insurance coverage he had signed onto as a financial professional. It ensured that if he were to suffer some major physical or mental distress while then employed, lifelong coverage was in place. He had certainly suffered that.

It was that insurance coverage that led George to me. Somewhere he had gotten enough money to go on a suicidal bender, and the doctors in Emergency told him that unless he received care, and that included psychiatric and/or therapeutic care, he would very likely end up dead. Despite what he said, he did not want to end up dead. He contacted the insurance people and requested therapeutic care; and the insurance people selected me purely at random. Nor was I their first pick—several others had already rejected him.

For all these reasons, I was not inclined to take George on. It wasn't an aversion to substance abuse cases as such—nearly everyone today has some substance-abuse-related issue, whether it 's fast food or too many anti-depressants.

But clients with *serious* substance-abuse issues—alcoholism, heroin and so on—are for the most part simply outside the effective conventional therapeutic range. Therapy is a conversational interaction that involves some degree of mental stability. Severe substance abuse causes physiological damage involving literal changes to the brain chemistry. A therapist cannot make headway until the substance-abuse is under control. Hence most therapists I know simply don't accept such patients.

Reviewing the information form from the insurance company and the George's medical data, I was not inclined to take him either.

And yet I did. I'm not sure to this day why I did, but I did. I had little hope I could do any good. Nonetheless I agreed to see him for one single session. After all, what did I have to lose? It was only one session.

I had no idea he would recover, completely, almost miraculously. No ideas that he would still be coming to see me years later, even to this day.

I remember that first meeting. George was striking. He was haggard and underweight, but he still had the remnant of his former good looks, and a strange dramatic quality, like an edgy method actor from an off-Broadway stage. He had the frightened and slightly frightening look of a person clearly at the end of his rope. His clothes were shabby, his hair unkempt, his face unshaven, his eyes wild.

And yet I noted that his shirt was properly buttoned, his posture consciously erect. He was clearly trying to hold himself together.

He was unhappy with his condition; he wanted to get better. I could see it in his face.

What was also visible was an incapacity to do so. He rocked, his hands would tremble, his voice would break, his blue eyes above the dark circles dart intensely around. His entire body language cried out: *crackhead!*

Yet the moment he spoke, that impression vanished: his language was articulate, precise, adult. Controlled. I had the impression that he was, or at least had been, a gentleman.

We spoke. He explained his situation. His failures. His losses. His poverty. There was no whining, and no self-forgiveness. He accepted full responsibility for what he was, and he despised what he was. He wanted to change.

At times there was a touch of sarcasm, of harsh bluntness. But on the whole, he spoke with dignity.

I felt for him. Why, I don't know, but I felt he could be reclaimed, and that he was worth reclaiming.

"I've been through multiple inpatient detox. Intensive outpatient programs. Sometimes I've been living in halfway houses, sometimes on the street."

"Are you in contact with your family?"

He laughed. Bitterly.

"No."

"Is there anyone who can help you with—."

There were tears in his blue eyes.

"There's no one who can help me with anything," he said. "No one except maybe you."

He put both his hands together and literally pleaded.

"Please. Can you help me, Doctor Pandey?"

For no reason I could put my finger on, I believed that I could.

For no reason I could put my finger on, I also believed in him. I believed he could change.

Why? I don't know. A therapist's intuition?

I certainly had no illusions about it being an easy process. I was honest with him. I told him that normally I believed in reducing the number of medications my clients took, gradually and with the help and cooperation of their primary physician. He would not have to go completely drug-free all at once, or ever—I had no objections to certain substances, like aspirin, vitamins, or a doctor's prescription for other health conditions.

But if he continued to take hard drugs, to drink, to indulge in the substance abuse that had more or less destroyed his life, then no: I couldn't help him. He needed to stop doing what he was doing. His drug usage had to come to a complete end, and he would need to reestablish a healthy physical baseline.

That was the first step.

He nodded.

"I understand."

George told me that even before he came to our first meeting, he'd decided to put his addiction completely behind him whether I took him on as a client or not. He talked about his children. His wife would not allow him to speak to them by court order, and they apparently showed no interest in reaching out to him on their own. He didn't blame them. But he did want, desperately, to reconnect with them, and for them no longer to feel ashamed of him.

The more we talked, the more hopeful I became. Strangely, for all the problems that he faced, George in some ways was remarkably problem-free. He seemed to have no childhood traumas to get over, no 'modern' problems like excess obesity or social media addiction, no destructive relationships to explore. Couples therapy was not required. He was not suffering from social maladjustment. He was entirely on his own—he had no social circle to adjust to.

He did still care for his family, and was deeply guilty over what he felt he had put them through. He hoped that his brother and sister and parents, whom he genuinely seemed to love, would eventually take a phone call. They would not take one now, and he had no intention of calling till he could present himself as some sort of semblance of his former self. He had no expectations that his wife would take him back.

Nor did he seem to have any goals. His career in investment banking was at an end. Period. He showed no sentimental nostalgia for his previous professional success. All that, he said, seemed a million miles away, parts of another life that belonged to another person, like a half-forgotten old movie that he vaguely remembered seeing.

But he did think constantly of his children, and of the burden of having so dysfunctional and embarrassing an excuse for a father. He felt was a cause for shame. And he was deeply ashamed.

"Shame is not a goal, George."

"What do you mean?"

"You can't escape from one frame of mind," I said, "without stepping into another. You say you want to escape your present way of life. But where do you want to *go?* If you don't want your children to be ashamed of you, then you must want them to be proud of you. For what, exactly? What can you do in the future that would inspire them to feel pride in you?"

He didn't answer. But he *thought* about my question. I felt that I could *see* him beginning to think in terms of the future again, in terms of accomplishments. New accomplishments.

From the moment he began to speak I felt a sort of faith in George. I felt that I could trust him. You feel that intuitively about certain clients. I don t know why.

I was deceiving myself.

We'd scheduled a meeting for next week.

George missed his session. I received a call from the local hospital instead. George had gone on a bender. One hell of a bender. He had locked himself in a motel room with as much alcohol as he could drink, and drank himself blind. At some point he had staggered out into traffic, reeling and howling, and then into the arms of the police. He woke up in detox.

That should've put an end to our sessions and our professional relationship. Normally it would have. Several days later I got a call from George virtually begging me to give him another chance and to let him come to another meeting.

Reason, statistics, common professional practice and sober clinical experience all counseled me to turn him down.

I shook my head no. I said yes.

Determined to do everything possible, I worked out a full formal intervention plan for George. I don't know why. To give myself the support of thinking I could apply a structured approach? Maybe.

In any event, I made a checklist. George and I, with a tip of our hats to B. F. Skinner, would work together to identify the antecedents (triggers), behaviors (drug/alcohol use), and consequences (positive or negative outcomes) associated with his substance abuse. We would set small, do-able, intermediary goals—wine instead of vodka! We would do proper Cognitive Restructuring: I would challenge George's maladaptive thoughts, beliefs, and attitudes, and replace his irrational or self-defeating ideas with more constructive ones. Meanwhile George would master the coping skills and relaxation strategies I would show him. He would learn to avoid high-risk temptations and situations. He would develop a support network, meditate mindfully, and breath from his lower abdomen while contemplating egolessness.

Oh, it looked so good on paper. Then George would come in and sit on the divan. I would begin to explain my structured approach in detail, and George would slump to his left and fall over onto the floor, unconscious, in a drunken stupor.

My plans were not entirely without value. Approaches and strategies did bubble up to the surface of our sessions now and again. George saw the sense in many of them, and even tried some of them, and when he did, he benefitted.

But we do not pass from chaos to order easily, and, for the most part, sessions with George were ragged and often painful. He felt tremendous guilt and shame. I would listen to every word because I knew that the expression of such shame was a first step in overcoming it and moving past it. Although time and again I would also make it clear that shame and guilt simply didn't help. So why indulge? What not ask what *would* help? The answer was not hard to arrive at: a goal, a purpose, using one's imagination to see and plan a constructive future, and then take action.

"Instead of dwelling on past mistake, George, stop for a moment. Look *ahead*. Look into the future. What do you see yourself there?"

"Dying of an overdose in the gutter."

I would put my face in my hand, and try again.

"Look deeper. What *possibilities* can you see there? What opportunities? Suppose you stopped drinking, stopped begging and panhandling, overcame your dependence on drugs. What be doing? What would you be thinking about?"

"Escaping back into drinking, begging, and drugs."

"Drugs and alcohol aren't a real escape: a *real* escape *leads* somewhere. Where do you want to *go?*"

"Back. Back before this whole nightmare ever

happened."

"You can't. You can't get your old life back again. You know that. But you *can* build a *new* life. You know *that*, too. What kind of a *new* life can you create? What kind of a life can you build now that would make your children feel proud?"

At times such questions would get through to George. I could see it. It was visible, and moving. At other times it was incredibly hard to get him to even think in terms of anything but the next drink. The worst danger was suicide. As our talks went on, I could see that his internal dialogue had devolved from an ever-running stream of self-criticism and self-abuse to a chronic whisper that he should simply end it all.

I tried to get him to examine that stream of words, that internal monologue. Not so much to refute it, at first, but simply to get him to recognize its lack of sense. Destroying himself would not make his children proud. Death would not reconcile him with his parents and siblings. Constantly putting himself down would not help him pick himself back up.

*What would?*

Sometimes he looked as though questions like these shot through to his very core. He would get up looking almost heroic, shoulders squared, ready to take on the world.

And then that evening I would get another call from a random detox center. George was back in rehab.

He crashed like that not once but eight times.

Each time I took him back and each time I promised myself that that time was the last. No client tested my patience more.

But I always agreed to see him. I tried to argue myself out of it. I told myself I could be using the time spent on George to provide therapy to someone who could genuinely benefit from it. George *wanted* to benefit from therapy, *seemed* to be on the point of genuine breakthroughs, and yet the moment he was out of the office I feared he would crash back down.

To his credit, most of the time, I was wrong. There would be weeks, months, of sobriety.

Then he would collapse back into the bottle or the needle again.

Sometimes he seemed not to even want to consider the possibility of a newer and better life. There were times when he came into the office reeking of alcohol. I would tell him to get out at once, and his face would crumple with embarrassment and remorse.

At other times, going over some of his experiences and memories, he would have screaming emotional fits such as I have seen in few patients. He would smash his fist into the wall, throw books out of my book case. Yes, he would threaten to attack me personally as well.

That was a line I did not allow him to cross. I would flatly *order* him out of the office immediately when that occurred. He would stare at me, place his head in his hands, break into tears, and go; and call back the next day deeply and sincerely and eloquently apologetic. The sincerity was such that I would accept the apology.

But accepting an apology isn't hope, and hopelessness can be addictive too. I had to remind myself that, if I refused to allow George to give in to despair over his chances of recovery, that I had no right to fall into it myself.

One of the things that clients don't always understand about therapists is that therapists to have to feel *hope* for their clients. It's not that we *want* to believe that our clients truly have the possibility of significant self-improvement. We *have* to believe that. Otherwise what is the point? This is why substance abuse cases are so destructive. They grind us down. We feel that our efforts have no effect. We seem to ourselves to be no more than way stations on a human being's path to self-destruction.

I just didn't feel that way about George. And I certainly paid for that gamble. Again: no client *ever* taxed my patience more. Americans have a saying: "Three strikes, you're out." After George's eighth strike I felt I had done enough. My efforts would better be directed towards people who could respond to them.

And yet I kept the door open for George. Why? All I can say is that between client and therapist there is a kind of intuitive resonance—the *attunement* that I speak of elsewhere. We come to *sense* that certain clients can be reached, just as they sense that they have reached a person whom they can trust, who will hear them, who will support them. I *knew* that George could recover.

And – he did!

I say that with joy and with amazement. He *did* recover! The lever appeared to be his love for his children. I believe that being able to see them again, being able to present a version of himself that they could respect and find tolerable, provided him the deciding motive force that allowed him to climb out of his abyss. He talked about regaining their respect often, and no line of discussion from George did I encourage more.

Returning to a drug-free lifestyle was like climbing a sheer high rock face for George, but apparently his work ethic from earlier days had survived: he climbed them, inch by inch. His drug use moderated, and then—stopped. I remember the day he looked at me and told me.

"It's over, Dr, Pandey. I'm done with all that. I'm just—done."

From a resident in halfway house, he eventually found himself becoming an employee. From an employee, he eventually became an administrator in their financial department. He certainly had the financial background!

It was not a job with a remotely comparable salary, but it paid enough to support him, and it was a meaningful job. One he's excelled at, and that brought him attention. A news story about the halfway house included George's story. Other prospective employers took note, and a few contacted him. He has career options again.

But George remains where he is—so far. Unemployment worries him. He remembers the street.

It doesn't worry him *too* much, though. Anxiety can be managed—that's what therapy is for.

To the mystery of why I stayed with George through all his ups and downs there remains another mystery. The mystery of why, one day, despite the odds, despite the statistics, he turned his back on his addictions, utterly and completely.

But he did. He remains clean to this day.

I call this chapter 'Success Story' because George to me exemplifies the ambiguous nature of success. Many people would consider the earlier George, the well-born, well-off, well-regarded financial expert rising to the peak of his profession to be the true success. Yet that very lifestyle, that environment, contained the seeds almost of his destruction. It was a Yin that contained a near-fatal Yang. A thesis that harbored a toxic, almost fatal, emergent antithesis.

Yet if George at his height was preparing himself for a plunge to the bottom, hitting bottom contained the seed of his resurrection: it was the speck of dust that created a pearl. At the lowest point, George somehow found the inner strength and discipline to pull himself together and return to a useful, productive, *compassionate* way of life, a life of helping and sheltering others.

For that I consider him one of my greatest successes, and I find his latter achievement to surpass anything he did in his previous career.

It's one thing to achieve the sort of external success we measure in dollars and cents. To develop the internal strength to overcome one's worst flaws, one's most corrosive cravings—that is an immeasurable achievement.

I said that George now has new career options. I didn't say what career he's been thinking of entering. He's more than competent at financial administration, but he's told me that he's considering counseling—specifically, counseling those with substance addictions. He knows the problems of people who've gone down the same path he himself once walked. He wants to help them, and he's uniquely positioned to do so.

It's a useful, humane, and poorly paying task. It isn't likely to bring him wealth. But then he tells me that he no longer confuses wealth with value. He's found value elsewhere. His former wife still refuses to see him, but George has found a Significant Other now too, and an attractive and intelligent one—his good looks have remained good enough for that.

His children are in college now, and they've met with him. He wrote them letters monthly since the day he went cold turkey forever. It was a homework assignment, and after many months they apparently began reading them—and writing back. He isn't a very close part of their lives. But he isn't utterly excluded from their lives either. He definitely has the experience needed to provide sound fatherly advice, and he does. He's joked to me that he's become the perfect model for his children: because of him, his children neither smoke nor drink nor take drugs. But they do invest. Successfully.

His parents? His parents are still alive, and like the parents in the biblical parable, rejoice in seeing their prodigal son return.

It is something of a cliché, and a dishonest cliché, to reduce America and its value systems purely to matters of money and business, as though financial success is the only measure of human merit. On sober reflection we all know that's silly. We don't consider Moses, Christ, Buddha, Plato, Shakespeare, great and towering figures because they could afford a fleet of Lamborghinis. None of them owned so much as a bicycle.

Yet it's hard for some of us to place a high value on a person with a low income. However great the person's spiritual achievement, if we can't see the material marks of that achievement, they remain all but invisible.

George is one of those people. His struggle to put aside multiple physical addictions forever for his children's sake, and for its *own* sake, is to me nothing less than heroic; an achievement that puts simple financial acumen in the shade. I watched every step. His failures and collapses broke my heart. His return from the depths, every single time, astounded me.

George hasn't passed beyond anxiety and certainly not beyond regret. He's no longer young, and worries getting older. But he no longer fears being old and alone. I'm almost tempted to say that he no longer *fears* at all. He's *aware* of his fears, his weaknesses, his cravings, his negative emotions. But he's no longer ruled by them. He's risen above all that.

George has passed from irresponsible greed

and terrible self-indulgence to responsibility and adulthood. Seeing how far he's come—seeing his *success*—fills me with pride.

.

## CHAPTER NINE

# EQUAL RITES

Wanda came to me badly in need of couples therapy. She came alone. She told me that she and her husband were deeply estranged. They'd been married for five years, and her husband, she said, had become verbally abusive, overbearing, domineering, and was sleeping with other women. Her husband refused to help in any serious way with domestic matters, refused to come with her to receive counseling, spent days and nights working at a highly paid corporate job, and was almost never at home any longer.

Wanda also had a job. A meaningful and often hectic one. But more and more, Wanda told me, she felt herself being demeaned, pushed, *crushed* into the role of traditional housewife.

It was not what she had bargained for when her partner had first proposed.

But somehow—*somehow*—she wanted to work things out.

I nodded sympathetically. I *was* sympathetic. Many of the couples I see in therapy follow exactly this pattern. The representative problem seemed clear enough: power dynamics. Equality in marriage is a noble ideal, but in practice traditional roles persist, and one of those roles is traditionally more powerful than the other.

I would have to meet her partner too, of course: there are two sides to every couple's story. But Wanda's description of her partner's behavior seemed a textbook example of toxic masculinity and male domination.

There was only one problem: her partner, Jackie, was a woman too.

Couples therapy for those in a same-sex marriage presents the therapist with curious challenges. In one sense, the same-sex angle would seem to have nothing to do with the problem at hand. Couples who argue too much, argue too much. The arguing is the problem, not the gender of the people arguing. If one partner is verbally abusive, or emotionally distant, or makes unwanted sexual demands, the problem is the abuse, the distance, the demand—the *behavior* of the person, not their gender.

A beginning therapist might conclude that one should deal with a same-sex couple in the exact same way that one would deal with any other couple. And—in a sense—that would be quite correct!

But also incorrect.

For the partners in a same-sex relationship face

pressures that partners in a more conventional marriage do not.

The surface problem is typically the one that the client most wants healed, but there are nuances under the surface that need to be considered for genuine healing to take place.

Also, where same-sex marriages are concerned, therapists are on novel ground. Therapeutic literature on same-sex marriage is almost in its infancy. Same-sex marriage was not even legal till June 26, 2015. It's true that a married couple remains a married couple, and that the problems and stresses that couples face remain much the same problems. Things are the same, yet, subtly, not quite the same. Both clients and therapists are navigating new yet strangely familiar shores.

Those shores are familiar enough to provide help to those who seek it, however. And Wanda was seeking it. So, we sat down in my office, and I listened to her story.

Wanda was the senior partner in the marriage. She was in her late thirties. (Jackie was twenty-eight.) I had her fill out a questionnaire, reviewed it briefly, and we spoke.

I was a little surprised to learn that, despite her apparent discomfort with the traditional role she claimed Jackie demanded that Wanda play in their household, Wanda's early upbringing was quite traditional. Moreover they were traditions to which she seemed quite friendly.

Wanda was Polish and had been brought to America at age two by parents concerned with the instability in East Europe at the time. They were practicing Catholics, but, like clumsy violinists, they didn't practice very much. Their church-going was lackadaisical to nonexistent. Wanda had been the religious one. She had even considered a religious vocation as a child. She did not like boys at all, much to her parents' approval—'Boys Are Trouble!'—and remained a virgin till college.

They had no idea that Wanda had lesbian leanings, and Wanda claimed not to have been particularly aware of any either. Certainly, she was not 'butch': her dress and manner were markedly what is commonly regarded as feminine. Her pale brown hair was long, her voice soft, her eyes kind, her manner sweet; she invariably wore skirts and dresses and stockings, never jeans or T-shirts. She was quite attractive in a way that bordered on a pronounced narcissism. Discussing her marriage, she said, offhandedly, that most of all she wanted "to be treated like a lady."

One would imagine that her religious and family background would make internal acceptance of her sexual orientation difficult. Whatever the reasons, that was not the case at all. In college, her church attendance dwindled as she fell into a long blur of marijuana usage that almost to her surprise merged into a string of shallow same-sex affairs.

She found herself regularly waking up from a hazy stupor in bed in the arms of other women. After a while she drew the conclusion that she was exclusively lesbian almost with a shrug. She informed her parents, who accepted the news with equal nonchalance, and supported her.

Being a lesbian didn't seem to change anything much about her life. She even continued haphazardly to go to Mass. Yes, she said, her sexual life was probably a sin, "but God doesn't really mind very much about these sorts of things, does He? Not if you live a good life otherwise."

Wanda *did* live a good life otherwise. At college she planned to train for a career working for charitable foundations. Her sexual orientation led her to expect that she would probably remain childless, but she had a particular delight in children, and a particular compassion for children with special needs. She switched her major in mid-course to Education, and by graduation she was qualified to teach. Her goal was to work with special needs children specifically, and that is what she did, well and happily.

Her switch in career direction coincided in with another major life event: meeting Jackie.

Contrary to rumor, opposites do not generally attract. Or rather, when they do, the attraction does not make for as natural or long-lasting a bond as common interests, common personality traits and high compatibility. So say the studies. But here as elsewhere, the studies didn't apply to Jackie and Wanda.

Jackie was *quite* different from Wanda, different even in the expression of their sexual orientation. For Wanda, her lesbianism was merely a curious fact. It didn't change her relationship to her parents or to God or to anything, really. It was just 'one of those things.'

Jackie, ten years Wanda's junior, was aggressively lesbian—aggressive, period, as well as determined and competitive and tough. Jackie was a Business Major at college and pursued her MBA passionately. She wanted to embark on a high-profile business career, reported Wanda, "and 'beat men at their own dirty game'."

Jackie, as Wanda described her, was sharp-tongued and short-haired. She wore male-flavored slacks and jackets. Her language abounded in phrases like 'power lunches,' 'hostile acquisitions' and 'extreme sports.' She was a "gym rat," pumping iron and running the treadmill with clockwork dependability.

Even as she talked about Jackie, Wanda seemed puzzled by their mutual attraction. I was too. From her description, power-lunch Jackie seemed to have nothing in common with the comparatively languid and feminine Wanda.

Yet for whatever reason their connection was—and remained—electric. Wanda had been "swept off her feet."

They met online, through a lesbian dating site. That very first meeting, Wanda was smitten by Jackie's dynamic personality, her vivaciousness and freedom.

They became inseparable. Within a few months, Jackie proposed that they move in together—that she wanted an exclusive, long-term relationship with Wanda.

Wanda felt in a trance. She didn't feel the need to 'think' about the next steps in this relationship, and she didn't think about them—she plunged in and abandoned herself to it. She let Jackie oversee the details of the relationship. She would close her eyes and resign herself to the sweet emotions of being with the 'perfect partner.'

Wanda wrapped up her studio apartment within weeks. Soon she was with Jackie at her luxurious downtown condo. Life was a free-flowing joy for them both. Wanda's schedule allowed her to embrace what she thought she wanted: the traditional role of wife, of domestic duties and caring for their home. She specifically wanted even the title: *wife*. (That was the last thing Jackie ever wanted to be called. 'Husband' and 'wife' became their tongue-in-cheek nicknames for one another.)

The first six months in the relationship, she said, was bliss. Both felt that they had found *the* special person, the one and only life partner, that they were a natural couple, fixed and eternal.

They formalized their bond. At the end of their yearlong courtship, they married. It was a joyous ceremony—for them. In other respects, it was somber affair. Most of Wanda's family was present, but not all. Jackie's parents and brother didn't attend at all—only had her younger sister, Bobbie. The couple's friends were there, but the absence, and implied censure of family, dimmed the proceedings for the newly married duo.

It was the first crack in the perfect relationship, but not the last. Early in their marriage, Wanda began to see Jackie's behavior patterns change. Jackie was traveling more; coming home late at night. And then, not coming home at all. Occasionally

Jackie would call—work dinners stretched late into the wee hours, and so Jackie was "sleeping in" at the coworker's apartment. Surely Wanda understood?

Wanda felt hurt and rejected, and more and more, she felt alone. Wanda began to regret her decision to rush the relationship.

But everything had been so perfect. Jackie was all Wanda ever wanted. Who else would ever love Wanda this much?

Wanda began blaming herself for the turn in their relationship. Jackie was so perfect, so smart, so extremely attractive. Women swooned over Jackie when they socialized; even men found her irresistible. She had looks, money, status.

What did Wanda have? Wanda didn't deserve her. And if things continued as they were going, she would lose her. Their relationship was failing. All the red flags were there to see.

But Wanda couldn't let things go. She wanted to salvage their marriage. An evening came when they sat down to dinner and Wanda gathered enough courage to have the difficult conversation she felt they both needed to have.

"Jackie," she said, "Darling... we're drifting away from each other. Growing distant."

"What are you talking about?" said Jackie.

"I know your work is important to you. I understand that. But you're putting your work first. Over me. Over *us.*"

Jackie, ever fiery, exploded.

"Wanda! Come *on!* You knew what you were walking into. My work *defines* me. My work is what

I *am*, and when I'm there, I'm there one hundred percent. One *thousand* percent! Sure, I feel bad about not being here with you more often. But I can't be everywhere all the time! Look at this place. Someone's got to *pay for* this lifestyle."

Wanda stood there shocked. Tears started to roll down her cheeks.

Jackie only got angier.

"I... I know your work matters to you, honey. I know you think it defines you. But our relationship defines *us*. We've created a life together! We need to put *us* over everything else, or... or all the rest just doesn't matter."

She wiped her eyes.

"I can't take this," snarled Jackie. "God! Either you talk or cry. You sound like some whining victimized straight wife on Oprah! As if it's all *my* fault! What am *I* supposed to do about it if you want to spend all day on some part-time feel-good 'career' and clean the house all day long?"

Wanda threw her glass of wine at Jackie. Jackie ducked. The glass shattered behind her. Dark Merlot trickled down the wall.

"*You* have problems with our relationship? What about *me?* It's *impossible* to take you out to a party. I've tried. You don't try to talk to my friends. The people I work with. You always want to go home."

The room became silent.

Wanda closed her eyes. Jackie looked away.

Wanda brushed her tears away. Minutes passed.

"Maybe we should talk to a professional," said

Wanda.

Jackie pushed her chair away from the table and stood up.

"I have no time for any of this therapy bullshit. If you think you have a problem and talking to someone will help, fine, great. Go for it. Send me the bill. Why not? *You* have all the time in the world to explore how perfect our relationship needs to be," said Jackie. "I don't have the time to waste."

Jackie's tone of voice was acid. Wanda was appalled. She excused herself and went to their bedroom and cried. Jackie slept in the guest room.

The next morning Wanda told Jackie she was going to make an appointment to speak to a couples therapist.

Jackie said nothing, finished breakfast, dressed, and went to work.

I nodded. That was the story—as told by Wanda. Was it the whole story? Probably not. "What's gone *wrong* with us, Doctor Pandey?" I couldn't answer that question after one visit, not without talking to Jackie too.

Besides, it wasn't a good question. "How can we get along better?" would have been a better one. Relationships evolve. Romantic incandescence can't glow at the same intensity forever. That doesn't mean that that precious light vanishes. Human emotions fluctuate. Isn't that true of everyone's experience?

Feelings have their peaks and valleys. Jackie and Wanda had drifted apart, and their relationship had entered that valley. That didn't mean their relationship couldn't recover. We break up; we make up; there is a rhythm to an enduring relationship, a rhythm that can strengthen that relationship as it learns to move past challenges.

But it's a dance that requires two partners. A good therapist *can* help one single partner in a couple that needs couples therapy. But it's vastly more effective to see them both, and to watch them interact. I told Wanda that I'd need to see Jackie too and gave her my relationship questionnaire for Jackie to fill out.

Wanda—using (she said) a Polish phrase that made me smile—told me that getting Jackie to fill it out would be like dragging a dead horse by the tail over a tall rocky hill. Getting her to agree to come to a session? That would be like dragging two dead horses over the hill!

But if it would keep them together, said Wanda, she'd find a way to make it happen.

She did. After four sessions involving only Wanda and myself, Jackie emailed me the relationship questionnaires. She also agreed to an individual session, to share her life and thoughts privately before committing to couples therapy.

I eagerly set Jackie up for the first available slot. I felt that her story would be fascinating.

It was. The moment she stepped into my office, I could see no point of resemblance to Wanda except one: a streak of narcissism too vivid to miss. She entered that first time in attire that could grace the cover of *Gentleman's Quarterly*. Her hair and nails and lipstick were exquisite, her figure fit and lithe, her posture erect and commanding. She obviously strove for effect and for attention.

That boded well. There are few places in life where one receives so much attention as a therapist's office. Narcissists love to talk about themselves, and as Jackie sat back and crossed her expensively stockinged legs and let her story unfold, she was hooked on having found so rapt an audience. As hooked as I was.

It wasn't a happy story. Far from it. Jackie had been born in the Deep South. Her parents were passionately religious Southern Baptists. From Jackie's description, their observance was nothing like the easy, lackadaisical, almost ironic Catholicism of Wanda's parents. Jackie's parents burned with hot intensity. Indeed, burning, hellfire, and damnation in a lake of flames were regular themes of Jackie's upbringing. Church attendance was frequent and mandatory, marked by speaking in tongues, spontaneous prophesy, pastoral screaming, the casting out of demons, miracle healings—evangelical flamboyance at its most extreme.

Unlike Wanda, Jackie seemed to be aware of her sexual orientation almost from the first, and she felt it as some awful flaw, as some squalid inherent evil in her nature—a curse from God. Which is how it was described (along with the eternal punishment to follow) in the Pastor's raging orations.

At ten, Jackie had succumbed, and kissed a fellow schoolgirl visiting her in her room, and the girl had kissed back. They continued, "in ecstasy" she said—till her mother entered the room.

The other girl got a violent slap across the face, and was sent home to her mother at once, with a promise that Jackie's mother would send word along as to why.

When Jackie's businessman father returned home and learned the news, he removed his belt and beat Jackie black and blue.

"Growing up," said Jackie that first session, smiling a huge, false, smile, "became an absolute nightmare. An absolute fucking nightmare."

"What happened next?"

She shrugged.

"What do you think? You can't whip a leopard into changing its spots, Doc. I kept finding pretty girls to kiss. My folks kept smacking me senseless. Till I was old enough to run away, anyway. I was sixteen."

Jackie recounted life as a runaway. Endless menial jobs that came and went. Lies about her age and pretending to be eighteen. The fear of being picked up by the police and sent home. The coarse attention and slimy propositions of pimps and crass old men. She drifted into a semi-call-girl lifestyle that even involved having sex with men. They reminded her of her father, and the experience was hideous.

"But it paid the bills," she said. Being selective about sexual partners was not a choice when the brutal alternative was poverty and destitution.

Living off the books and hiding from authorities, she became aware of another world on the fringes—the world of drugs and drug-dealing.

But Jackie was too tough, and too smart, to fall

for that. She analyzed her situation, saw that she was going nowhere, and concluded that the only thing that would take her somewhere better was money. Not the immediate cash she got from men and from selling weed, from washing dishes and cleaning toilets, but the long-term mastery of money, a mastery embodied in the occasional successful businessman patron she serviced They had mastered the fine art of getting money and growing more money. Jackie ached to gain that mastery.

It came at a price: she needed to get an education. She got an education. She lived on pennies, saved up all she could, and even built little businesses of her own, getting tiny handyman jobs or house cleaning calls and then hiring others to do the work and split the fee. Eventually she built a small crew of employees. Eventually one homeowner using her services who ran a business saw and liked her aggressiveness.

He made her a job offer—secretarial work. She declined. She pressed him to let her work with his people in sales. Amused, he agreed. The overly young intense saleswoman proved an unexpected hit with his clients. She started to make money. Serious money.

The first thing she did with it was pay for a gym membership and a personal trainer. At home she had been beaten into obedience and conformity to authority. So, in high school she channeled all her anger, all her rebellion, all her sexual energy into sports. It had left her fit and athletic—the one area in life where she felt successful and in full self-control.

She wanted that feeling again. Because now she had enough to put herself through school. A top-tier Chicago business school that had no room for penniless runaways or hustling Southern trash. She needed to remake herself—to exercise self-control as never before.

College was a new world for Jackie. And the most amazing thing about that new world was how many other young women there shared her own sexual orientation. But not her guilt, or shame, or the subliminally persistent theological dread. She immersed herself into the university's gay community like a pearl diver plunging into the depths.

But the pearl she was looking for wasn't simple sexual self-indulgence. Like Wanda, she over-indulged considerably. But the politics and feminist rhetoric left her cold, and sexual self-indulgence alone was empty. She wanted more; she wanted emotional satisfaction too; she wanted to satisfy soul as well as body.

Then she met Wanda. Who, to Jackie, was the embodiment of femininity, of gentleness and beauty. But more than that: someone who seemed free of the need to struggle desperately, to hide, to fear.

Who seemed *free*.

The more I spoke to the couple, the more I noticed an odd dynamic. Wanda, nine years Jackie's senior, seemed to dote on Jackie in an almost motherly way. Jackie, in turn, showed an emotional dependence that was both touching and yet rebellious—even juvenile.

"You're not my mother!" she would bark at

Wanda. Which, of course, suggested that that is exactly what she represented to Jackie, for that is exactly how Jackie treated her. From the outside, Jackie seemed the directive partner, but in the interior landscape of the relationship, Jackie's anger was far closer to that of a resentful child.

There was a similar inversion in Wanda's manner. She had presented me a picture of Jackie acting almost autonomously, raining manipulation down on her without cause or reason.

But seeing them interact, it was impossible to miss the *passive*-aggressive manipulations issuing regularly from Wanda. Jackie would complain in her blunt, blatant, direct way, but Wanda would meet those remarks with glances and frowns and body language Arctic in their iciness. Wanda's way of speaking was typically soft and musical, but she had a way of using her tone of voice to mark certain words with the most acid contempt. "Of *course,* you're right, *Darling,*" her words would say, while the *tonality* screamed, "How dare you say that to me, you bitch!"

Their interactions were like a stylized ritual, different in manner, but similar in cruelty. It was startling to see how easily and how regularly Wanda could *hurt* Jackie. Jackie's crude foot-stamping barely approached it in savagery.

I'm sometimes asked how a therapist can give total attention to her clients. The answer is simple. They're fascinating! Listening to Jackie and Wanda interact was like watching a brilliantly written New York stage drama unfold. The palpable love they felt for one another, the anger repressed and expressed, the gross and subtle mutual arm-twisting, the nuanced manipulation—it was dazzling.

Dazzling enough to make me force myself to return to planet earth. These clients had come to me saying they were experiencing a problem. What specifically was that problem? How could I help? That's what I was here for.

True, they were a same-sex couple. Were their sexual orientations a factor in the problems? Did it worsen the problem, did it make things easier? Did it complicate treatment? How? In what ways?

The couple's problems were several. But the key problem was obviously power dynamics, expressed through the medium of finance. Jackie was in a high-level sales position with a major corporation making a great deal of money. Wanda taught disabled children and made very little.

As the partner that donated the most money and paid most of the bills, Jackie felt that made her the senior partner. Work came first, domestic relations second. *Wanda* should handle the domestic duties, not Jackie, the hard-charging sales professional burning the midnight oil.

Wanda responded that her job took just as long as Jackie's and was no less important—"Does a *child* matter less than selling some stupid widgets?"

Interestingly, these power relations were reversed in their jobs.

Jackie had almost no control in her position. Her sales targets were given to her, and she was completely dependent on her prospect, who could turn thumbs up or down on a sale on a whim.

By contrast Wanda was absolute master in her classroom, directing the children as she pleased.

As time passed, I came to think of Jackie's attempted power grabs in the home as being a form of overcompensation—she needed to exercise power *somewhere*. But Wanda was no victim. She exercised power over her charges every day, and her quiet but hard-headed determination to continue to extend the power she exercised over those in her care at home and over Jackie was clear.

In those first talks, everything revolved around domestic duties. Each wanted the other to do more about the house. The solution seemed obvious: hire more help. Jackie could certainly afford it. It even made financial sense for her. The more time it opened up for her, the more she could sell.

But not *psychic* sense. Both wanted the other partner to *submit*, to *concede*; to admit the contribution and the worth, the *greater* worth, of the other.

And this, I think, was where sexual orientation *was* a relevant factor. Homophobia, we all know, is a reality. Gay people suffer in ways ranging from occasional violent persecution to discrimination, avoidance, condescension, and petty slights. What each such person experiences varies, but both Wanda and Jackie had the self-esteem issues that are part and parcel of being a marginalized minority.

Clearly Jackie had had a much harder time of it than Wanda, and she wanted—demanded! —an acknowledgement of her worth, her *achievement*.

Wanda had far less of a self-esteem issue, but

she also had enough self-esteem not to let Jackie chip away at what Wanda considered her equal position. She was, after all, the elder partner, and the caregiving one. She made less money, but that did not make her less valuable, which is how she interpreted Jackie's demands.

She appreciated Jackie's financial contributions to the household, but in the end money-grubbing was petty money-grubbing. And anyway, "A husband is *expected* to pay the bills." Besides, money was the root of all evil, and helping the disabled was, well, *Christian*.

I could hear Jackie's teeth grind.

While the two clearly loved each other, I was struck by the lack of mutual insight, the struggle for position. I'd worked with two other same-sex couples, both males, and in those cases I was surprised at an easy-going equality between them. Heterosexual males and females famously go on about the incomprehensibility of the other: *"Men come from Mars, women come from Venus!"* But in the male same-sex couples I'd treated, each male partner appeared to understand the other pretty well. They didn't seem to have much of a problem dividing up domestic duties or financial expenditures. Equality simply seemed to be a sort of given. Why not? They were both men!

With Jackie and Wanda, however, *in*equality, like their overly pronounced masculinity and femininity, seemed to be not only the norm but a kind of goal. Jackie wanted to ever more dominate, while Wanda played even more at being the (subversive) female 'victim.'

Magazine-stand pop psychology holds (formal psychology is nowhere near as simple-minded) that in gay relationships one partner takes on the male stereotype and the other the female. The standard nuclear family model is presented as a kind of mental template to which even gay couples conform.

That hasn't been my experience with male gay couples. The ones I've seen seemed to me very egalitarian—'partners' without qualification.

But I would *not* generalize about all male same-sex relationships from the cases I personally have handled, and I would certainly *not* generalize about all female same-sex relationships from the single case of Jackie and Wanda. Nonetheless their particular relationship seemed not only to conform to stereotype but to push the stereotypes further.

Is that a common distinction between male and female same-sex married couples? I leave it to researchers and statisticians.

Where Jackie and Wanda were concerned, however, both called for equality, but equality was not the real goal driving either. Their relationship had become a strange sort of power struggle where the specific demands were demands for concessions. Concessions not insisted upon because of their intrinsic value, but for the self-affirmation that the other's concession provided. Wanda wanted Jackie to *show* that Jackie valued her as an equal partner.

Jackie wanted Wanda to *concede* that she was giving more, doing more, contributing more, working harder.

Why the need for confirmation? I came to think of it as a reflection of that internal struggle for self-acceptance that some gay individuals may face. The homophobia they experience, real or assumed, demeans them. Repeated long enough, often enough, subliminally in thousands of quiet ways, and such homophobia becomes internalized. Few egos are so strong as to repudiate such a concerted barrage by sheer force of will. Most people need the outer world, or some part of the outer world, to affirm their value, their sense of self.

In the case of Jackie and Wanda, each wanted—and had found—that affirmation from the other. But it needed constant reinforcement. Concessions concerning domestic matters were symbolic ways each could re-state something each needed to hear constantly restated.

The problem also was that other of their behaviors were sending quite the opposite message. For instance, adultery. Jackie's sales trips involved a good deal of time spent in distant cities. Jackie admitted to engaging in liaisons there—and Wanda was alone during her partner's long trips. Was she expected to just sit there by herself? Why couldn't *she* find some brief companionship too? She admitted that she did.

Neither rubbed their adulteries in the other's face. Both said that they were proud to have an open, mature marriage, and lied that they were not hurt by the other's actions. They were hurt, and resentful, and the resentments festered.

Eventually Jackie's other relationships began to draw her away from Wanda, and Wanda's companions began to draw Wanda away from Jackie.

Arguments flared, and became explosions.

The relationship deteriorated, and threatened to die.

They looked to me for a solution, but the problems were deeper than they appeared. Still, they were the sort of deep problems that behavior therapy excels in providing—for a while: shallow-seeming but helpful behavioral fixes.

Could Jackie go on fewer long-distance trips, I asked? Yes, she said.

Would Wanda like to see more of Jackie? Yes.

I suggested that Jackie ask her sales manager for fewer long-distance assignments.

She did, and got them.

Did the couple bond more closely as a result? Yes.

Therapy is not always rocket science.

Disagreements still happened. Shouting still occurred. But less often.

More objective conversations helped too. Upon mindful reflection, most of us can see the difference between an appropriate emotional reaction and an inappropriate over-emotional one, between a reasonable assessment and an unreasonable one.

"Jackie," I would say, "do you *really* think sales is a more valuable job than caring for disabled children?"

"It pays the bills!"

"Yes, it does. And that matters. Wanda, would you agree?"

Wanda would frown and purse her lips, but then she would shrug, and say, "Yes." She would look over at Jackie and say, "Yes. I appreciate all that you do, Jackie."

Jackie would say nothing. Then, "Your work matters too, Wanda. I know that. It's just that... You don't understand. I'm under so much *pressure* at work!"

"Wanda?" I would say. "Do you agree with Jackie that she really is under considerable stress at times? Have you seen any evidence of that?"

"I see it all the time," Wanda would say. "I know things are tough on Jackie sometimes. I wish she would be more open about it. And not just keep it bottled up till she blows up."

These were small concessions, incremental acknowledgments. But, alongside the reduction in arguments, along with other tiny changes and sober reflections, the self-exploration of our meetings took the edges off their conflict.

Strange to say, love, even passionate love, is not the same thing as empathy. A mutual *empathy* now began to grow between them. Between them, and beyond them.

One day my phone rang. It was Wanda.

"Dr. Pandey?"

"Yes, Wanda," I said. "What is it?"

"Could we schedule an extra session this week? Jackie wants to talk to you."

"Is it about something important?" I asked, curious.

"It's important to Jackie," she said. "Very important."

There was a spot open the next day. I scheduled it.

The couple came in on the dot. They sat on the sofa together, and Wanda held Jackie's hand.

"Has something happened?"

"Jackie contacted her family," said Wanda.

"It was pure impulse," said Jackie, petting Wanda's hand. "I was having lunch at a bistro. You know, the one on North Oak Park? Hemmingway's. I ordered a meal and got out my Samsung to make yet another sales call."

"And?"

"I found myself dialing my parents. It was like my fingers were dialing their number by themselves. It just seemed to happen. My Mom picked up.

"Hello?" she said.

"Mom?" I said. "Mom. it's me. Jackie."

Her mother began to cry and called her father over at once.

Jackie's father took the phone.

"Honey?" he said, the voice older now, and cracked. "Honey. How are you?"

Jackie told her parents that she was in good health, that she was doing well financially—and that she was still married to the same woman.

She steeled herself, expecting her father to hang up.

But he didn't. They talked around the subject, but they talked. Then her mother took the phone, and they talked too.

The family still did not accept her sexual identity, of course. They remained the extremely religious people they had always been. Her parents had been married to each other for over thirty-five years now, and to them, marriage was a sacrament between a man and a woman. All else was sin.

Like Jackie, her parents were people of will. Call or no call, it had to be said, and her father said it.

"You can change, honey" her father half-pleaded, half-demanded.

"I don't want to change, Poppa," said Jackie. "I am who I am." She added, in a whisper, "*You* can change too. You don't have to shut me out."

Her father was silent. Her mother took the phone again.

"We've never shut you out, Jackie. The door is always open. Come see us! We want to see you again. Both of us."

Jackie slowly hung up.

"There's a business conference coming up," said Jackie. "It's not far from the town where I was raised. I could set up a visit. I guess."

"Should I go, Doctor Pandey?" she asked.

"Go," I said.

Jackie arranged the visit—a visit with her parents for the first time in years.

After she returned, we discussed it in my office, Wanda holding her hand the same way. Jackie, normally brassy and direct, was at a loss for words, almost confused. The huge house she remembered was small, the rooms neglected, the roof needed repair. The parents she remembered as massive shouting figures towering over her, were older now, white-haired, quieter, smaller. The car she arrived in, her clothes, her manner all spoke of her success and her prosperity. Their own small means stood in stark contrast.

But they welcomed her in, and hugged her. Inevitably too, as she was sure they would, they called on her to repent, and broke into prayer for her on the spot.

But this time Jackie didn't see it as coercive. She saw two old people that, after all, genuinely seemed to care for her, two people who sincerely prayed for the good of her soul; as they had, they told her, every day since she left.

They loved her, she realized. They did not know *how* to love her very well, perhaps, but they loved her.

She was moved; shaken. When she returned to Wanda in Chicago she broke down in tears in Wanda's arms.

The visit changed something in Jackie. At Wanda's suggestion, she arranged that some of Jackie's considerable funds went to her parents. Not cash. "They'll just hand it over to their Church," said Jackie. But a non-transferable line of credit at the grocery story, a new pick-up truck (In Jackie's name). Her parents, and only her parents, might get some use out of that.

The new generosity spilled over: now if Wanda made some reasonable purchase for their Chicago home and charged it to Jackie's account, the usual financial squabble never happened. "That's fine," Jackie would say.

The change went in the other direction too. Wanda confessed during a visit that she had always felt a certain discomfort about her relationship with Jackie, because Jackie, she felt, had given up so much.

Wanda had always had, and had always retained, the love of her family. Marrying Wanda cut Jackie off from her family forever—or so Wanda had thought. She felt that had forced Jackie to give up too much—and resented the guilt that came with it. That separation was now dissolving; and with it, Wanda's unspoken guilt.

Jackie admitted to guilt feelings of her own. Wanda had such an obvious love of children. She would never have her own, of course, not with Jackie as her partner. Jackie felt she was cutting Wanda off from a fulfillment that could have meant a great deal to her.

"Have either of you considered adoption?" I asked. They looked at one another. As with so many issues in couples therapy, unfaced and unmentioned issues sometimes have more weight and presence than the issues discussed—until they *are* faced and discussed.

A few years have passed since I first began seeing the couple. I did see them recently, and there seems a growing fullness to their relationship now.

It was not one thing that led to that greater full-ness, but small things and small steps, from airing their grievances honestly, sharing their unspoken thoughts, fostering more self-examination, giving time to mindful reflection, from little assignments like Wanda visiting Jackie's office, and Jackie visit-ing Wanda's school and meeting the children, to large steps like a phone call and a visit to estranged parents.

But in time all the small pieces come together, and enough small steps take you to the place you want to be.

Jackie and Wanda continue to see me now and again. They still have disagreements, but the disa-greements aren't pressing. No, they don't live to-gether in idyllic perfection. Who does? But they don't experience the rancor, the unstated demands and resentments and guilt that were there before. Those things have faded away, as they generally do when expressed and examined, and when action is taken to alleviate them.

Have Jackie's parents accepted her orientation? No. But they love her regardless and say so and keep in touch.

Do Jackie and Wanda argue? They disagree. But now they come to terms, and know how to come to terms, standing up where it is reasonable to stand up and yielding gracefully where it is reasonable to yield. Aggressive demands and passive-aggressive pushback are no longer the default strategies. As they both have come to see, those approaches simply don't work.

Have Jackie and Wanda adopted? Not yet. Perhaps they will. Perhaps not.

Do I consider the therapy to date successful? I do.

I also consider it a case worth sharing because of the strange grip of political correctness in the therapeutic field nowadays. How was I to provide effective therapy to a same-sex married couple? One ideological school argues that one should treat them as uniquely special, as oppressed people for whom normal therapeutic strategies simply don't apply. An opposing school argues that therapists should ignore the same-sex aspect completely—that all couples are couples, not fundamentally different, and should be treated the same way.

The problem with both approaches is that they deal with theories and not living individuals.

What I learned from Jackie and Wanda is not exactly that the best way is the middle way, though it often is, but that certain problems—different expectations, matters of stress and class, unstated guilt, stifled resentments, parental acceptance or rejection—are *human* problems, regardless of gender. Every couple experiences them.

Gay couples may have a different, added weight, different *emphases*, that color those problems, and that need to be considered for optimal treatment. But the problems are not fundamentally different, nor are the solutions. Mindfulness, empathy, mutual compassion, forgiveness, careful attention to behavior, benefit all relationships, not only heterosexual ones.

Every therapeutic problem is a *particular* problem. General solutions apply, but they need to accommodate the individual situations of the clients. Jackie and Wanda opened a window for me into the psychological life of gay couples, and into the unique abrasions they face in society and how they internalize those abrasions.

But that said—even with all its abrasions, life remains precious. With a little thoughtfulness, it can even be enjoyable. Even fulfilling.

Freud used to speak of 'transference,' by which he referred to the romantic fixation a patient sometimes develops for a therapist. I would like to propose a 'transference' of my own: a transference of behavior from therapist to client.

For example? Jackie told me had never felt acceptance as a person (at least in the total way Carl Rogers presents it) till our sessions. Wanda loved her, to be sure, but Jackie was nothing if not exasperated by her orders and demands. Like Jackie's parents, Wanda wanted Jackie to change. Even Jackie wanted Jackie to change. I didn't. I wasn't there to judge, or coerce, or mandate. I wanted only to hear her story.

Speaking to a therapist who could accept her entirely as she was, differences and all, was a new experience for Jackie. Over time, I believe, Jackie learned to do the same thing—to extend acceptance to her parents, for instance, despite their continuing non-acceptance. Seeing Jackie's forgiveness and tolerance inspired something of the same in Wanda's feelings toward Jackie.

Therapists do not simply modify behavior: they also model behavior. They present ways of interacting with clients that radiate outwards and further outwards, benefiting not just the client but others—many others. It's a transference passed down to this therapist from Carl Rogers and Aaron Beck and so many of our profession's esteemed predecessors. And sometimes, as it passes from them to us and then beyond ourselves to our clients and through them to others, I sometimes think I can see far away the beginnings of a truly healthy, sane society.

How far away? Only time will tell.

## CHAPTER TEN

# DISCARNATE

I often find therapy to be a pleasure.

That may surprise you. Quite a few people think of therapists as groaning under the tough emotional burden of having to see deeply troubled people with severe personal challenges all day.

In fact, many of the clients I see are quite decent, individuals—amiable, witty, interesting, sympathetic. Moreover, when a patient comes into my office, I feel confident. Even eager. I'm reasonably sure that the person will be someone I will enjoy meeting and knowing, and someone whose problem I can very likely help resolve, for I may well have alleviated a similar problem for another client in the past.

After all, aside from my own experience, there are hundreds of thousands of case studies detailing successful resolutions of common client problems. I rarely come across a case that seems genuinely novel, a case that hasn't been successfully addressed in the profession many times.

So when a new client appears, I feel rather sure that I can help them, just as many people in their situation have been helped before. I'm also reasonably sure the person I'm about to deal with is someone fairly personable, or at the very least not *inexplicably* unpleasant.

With the client I will call Greta, none of that applied. I found myself operating on entirely new ground.

Greta had had an unusual upbringing. She was born in East Germany to an unwed mother just before its collapse. After that nation's fall, her parents moved to West Germany where the marriage itself collapsed. The mother took young Greta and immigrated again, this time to Brazil, where she married a widowed insurance salesperson with four older children. The man's company went out of business, so he and Greta's mother decided to take the new family to the United States, where they stayed even after their visas expired.

The contradictions of being an East German girl from an East Germany that no longer existed, and of being a member of a Hispanic family without being Hispanic, and of living in yet a third country where her status as a citizen was legally ambiguous, all made Greta's childhood quite fascinating to me. She was an immigrant, like me, but unlike me she was without a cultural identity passed down to her. If anything, it had been repeatedly stripped away.

Greta struggled almost from birth with a sense

of not belonging. Her four Brazilian siblings, she told me, had never really accepted her as a sister, and didn't seem to adapt well to their new nation either. They dropped out of school at the earliest opportunity, as soon as they grew old enough to enter the American workforce. But they made no mark in it, vanishing into the fast food and service industries.

The foster father she described was something of a narcissist: a bluff vivid figure forever inflating his importance and bragging about business opportunities that never quite seemed to materialize. He left Greta's mother soon after his own children departed, and by then Greta's mother had died in an auto accident.

Greta was on her own. But had no regrets about it. She landed on her feet, and began working towards a university degree.

At school she thrived. Or rather—for it would not be quite accurate to say that Greta thrived emotionally—she excelled. Greta had *sitzfleisch*: the ability to put herself into a chair and study for hours upon hours. It did not make her popular— she joined no clubs, no sororities, she rarely partied or dated. But she did master her subjects, earned excellent grades, and was soon a skilled graduate with a much-sought-after degree in computer science.

She entered the workforce immediately upon graduation. But not, like her vanished expatriate siblings, in the services industry. She was making six figures out of the box as a programmer and security systems analyst.

During one gig for an up-and-coming startup, Greta met and married a Jewish attorney specializing in intellectual properties. He was several years her senior, and the two soon had a child. The husband joined a major Chicago law firm, taking a less than major position for what he thought would be greater job security. Greta herself joined a Big Tech firm based in Chicago as a software consultant. She rapidly became very successful, almost indispensable. She'd been working there for six years when she and I first met.

She insisted that we first meet online. It was 2020, the year the Pandemic broke. ear of COVID was already forcing many formerly face-to-face meetings with therapists into Zoom sessions. Still, I was reluctant. I preferred meeting in person. A meeting online was a meeting one step removed.

She was insistent, however, so we connected on Zoom as she asked. It was not an auspicious meeting. She had been recommended to me by a psychiatrist, who explained to me that she was already on medications. On a great variety of medications.

That wasn't good news. Prescribed psychiatric drugs often had negative side effects, and I'd seen cases where cocktails of prescribed psychiatric drugs were worsened by other over-the-counter drugs, or illegal or recreational drugs that clients might not always admit using, despite warnings not to mix them with prescription medication.

Even with Zoom reducing what I could see of her and her body language, my first sight of her reinforced that intuition. She looked disheveled. Her hair needed cutting. She wore no makeup, there were circles under her eyes. She would look around herself suspiciously with sharp, nervous glances, pull at her hair, and work her hands in an anxious irritable way.

As we spoke, she seemed hostile, almost on the edge of panic; aggressive yet unable to collect her thoughts. She glanced about the office, and at me, with a nervous anger. Soon I would see that fuming anger burst into outright ranting paranoia, but even at this first meeting Greta's instability was vivid and unmistakable.

I had to consider that I might be reading too much into her reactions. After all, Greta had come to me as the COVID panic was beginning to peak. Much of the nation was already in lockdown, protests were happening in hundreds of American cities, and the 2020 election frenzy was in full swing. If she appeared to be under stress, why shouldn't she be? So were millions of others.

I introduced myself with a few lines of small talk and then explained to her that I liked to begin with a brief personal interview and then have the client answer the questions on an assessment form.

"Fine. *Fine*," she said. "Ask your questions. *Do* it."

I began asking questions and tried to gather information. It wasn't easy. She was all over the place. We've all seen people who haven't gotten enough sleep, and also people who talk too fast. Greta was both. What she said wasn't always coherent, and was occasionally mumbled, but the words spilled out a mile a minute. I'd ask a question and she would ramble on in a rushing stream of consciousness, darting from subject to subject as though content itself was a nervous tic.

Some potentially relevant things emerged—her son was five but not at school, owing to the school lockdowns. His schooling was now in his parents' hands. Her husband might have been of some help there, but he'd been furloughed from his business, and was himself falling into depression. He felt it was a temporary lockdown matter and that he'd called back, but time was passing, and no call came.

Greta was suspicious: she was convinced he'd lost his job permanently and was lying to her. She was suspicious of the people at her *own* company, despite her importance there, and felt they were maneuvering to remove her, too.

The fear and paranoia she radiated were almost tangible and (as I gradually found) informed many of her physical symptoms: shortness of breath, inability to eat, constant anxiety, chronic exhaustion.

A major in the initial session was her lack of trust and paranoia. She looked at me in a cagey, skeptical manner. She asked three times whether I was recording the session, or if there was another person there in my office. I assured her that there was no recording going on and there was no one in my office. She asked me to move my laptop around so the camera would confirm it.

This was something uncommon in my outpatient practice so far. I declined. I did not want to start our relationship out by bending to a rather paranoid request. What would she ask for next, my driver's license? I again assured her that I took patient confidentiality very seriously, and that no one would have access to our conversation or my notes without her consent. But she would have to give me *some* measure of trust if our talks were to have any worth.

She stared at me through the screen. Her unkempt looks, constricted affect, pressured speech, all made me wonder if there was possibly an underlying psychosis.

"Yeah, OK, whatever." She waved her hand dismissively.

I tried to redirect her attention to the problem that had brought her here. I used a crafty therapeutic stratagem: I asked her.

"What brought you here, Greta?"

She snorted.

"Management. They insisted. *Fascists!* They say my 'performance' has been 'erratic.' I need to 'talk' to someone. Yeah, I need to talk to someone, all right. About *them*. My managers. They're ganging up on me. Conspiring against me. Bastards. *Racist scum.*"

I was confused. Greta did not seem visibly to belong to any historically persecuted minority. Why the accusation of racism?

I tried to bring her into "here and now" and shifted the focus to her daily life.

"Tell me about yesterday," I said. "When did you get up?"

"5 am. Maybe 4 am. I don't know."

"What did you do next? Shower? Breakfast with the family?"

She scowled at me.

"I don't have time for that *crap*. I have to get

online as soon as I'm awake.

"Why? Are you expecting an important email?"

She sneered. "No, I have to check various organizer sites that I oversee. I *have to*. I support several activist causes. Social justice causes. You know what those are, right? The election's almost here and no one knows what's going to happen. There's looting in Chicago and cops are killing people. You understand? People are getting *killed*. Someone has to raise peoples' awareness about uniting, organizing, fighting the power."

"And that someone is you.? "

"Why *not* me?" she said. "*Someone* has to. *Someone* has to do something. We can't just sit and watch the destruction. *People are dying!* There's fighting in the streets. Oppressed people taking power into their own hands. Seizing power!"

She made a fist and lifted it into the air."

"The rich, the people exploiting us, exploiting everyone, they think people are weak. They don't understand. They don't have a clue. We're living in the age of the internet now. We can *connect*. We can *organize*. Thanks to the net *I* can do something. I can raise peoples' consciousness, form groups, connect people to take charge and *do something*, and we *have* to do something, because the current government is a bunch of crazy blood-sucking psychos."

"So that's what you have been doing lately? Organizing?"

Her eyes gleamed.

"I have organized nine—*nine*—different group fighting for justice and fairness. And there are other fighters like me, other organizers I religiously follow on Instagram. We're getting *real work* done, making *real advances* towards saving humanity."

I nodded.

"How many hours a day do you spend on these groups and on social media in general?" I asked.

Her face emitted a nervous tic.

"I don't know," she said. "Nine, ten hours."

"Every day?"

"Sometimes twelve hours." She shrugged. "Sometimes fourteen."

*Fourteen hours a day on social media?*

A smile crossed my face.

It was a mistake. She became furious.

*"Don't roll your eyes at me like that!"* she shouted.

"I'm just puzzled," I said. "You have a five-year-old child at home who needs your care. Your husband isn't working. No one is going out because of the lockdown. Don't you think you should be spending more time with them at home?"

"Well... who's going to bring the bread home, Dr. Pandey? I'm the sole breadwinner now, and I do my company work each day."

"Yet on top of your work, you still manage to spend fourteen hours a day on social media? Where do you get the time?"

She smiled and drew a loopy finger across the screen.

"Oh, you can always find the time. There are ways around the bosses. Around work. If you're smart."

"But your family... "

She brushed my question aside entirely, and suddenly launched into a long political diatribe. How could you expect people to get energized and do anything about genocide, poverty, racism, hate, she asked, if no one ever got through to them and reached them? If people didn't go online and organize, and network, and raise public consciousness?

Her comments sounded more like accusations than conversation, and her sentences were peppered with intense stock phrases I'd heard on the news: "Speak truth to power. Be the change. Make it happen. Justice. Payback. No human being is illegal. Black lives matter."

I could hardly disagree. After all, black lives *do* matter. Whose life doesn't? Greta was an immigrant, so was I. The lives of immigrants mattered a great deal to me as well.

But she didn't linger on those subjects, or any subject. She transitioned quickly from one cause to the next, from climate change to LGBTQ+ rights, from genocide to slavery to poverty, from police brutalizing black bodies to children languishing in cages on the border.

The name of Donald Trump came up constantly, invariably couched in the most extreme vitriolic obscenities. Indeed, the almost *personal* relationship she had mentally established with Trump was striking. It was not an opposition to his policies so much as an incandescent hatred, a total and utter personal revulsion, for the person himself. I'd ask her about her husband and her five-year-old son, and she'd shrug, and mumble something about them briefly, almost in passing. She seemed almost indifferent. But if the name Donald Trump came up, she became furious, screeching, livid.

"Is that all you talk about on social platforms all day? Just politics?"

"*Just* politics? There are people in this city right now, protesting on the streets. *Fighting in the streets*, Dr. P! The police are *shooting and killing* people in the streets. How can you sit there and support that?"

"I don't support shooting or killing anyone."

"Then you agree with me! *You* think they should defund those pigs too!"

"But what happens if your house is looted, or some criminal decides to attack you?"

That kind of response got her even angrier. "Those are *fascist* talking points," she would say. "Are you a *Republican* or something?"

"Our meetings are not about me, Greta. I do have personal opinions about various topics. But I don't bring them to client conversations. During therapy I don't have any political opinions."

"*Silence is violence!* Don't you *care?* Don't you know *what's going on?*"

That first session, and several to follow, was one long shouting match. Or perhaps I should say one long assault, with Greta doing the shouting. Greta kept trying to trap me into agreeing with some political statement she would make, or to get me to confess to some right-wing leaning she felt I was hiding. I would try to slip her punch by informing her calmly that I was there to help her with her private life, period, not to engage her in abstract discussions. This would enrage her, and she would become even more infuriated.

Most times, and that first time as well, she stormed out of the conversation and logged off. I sat there looking at a blank screen and doubted I would ever see her again.

But I would get an email soon after to schedule another session and to my surprise, an apology (of sorts) for getting upset and logging off so abruptly. There was so much injustice in the world, so much greed, so much evil. It got her "too worked up" and made it hard for her to process her thoughts. She wasn't embarrassed or contrite. She wasn't to blame. The world was to blame. The world needed to change, not her.

Greta was on time religiously for the next session, and for every session for the next six months. Many of those early sessions ended the same way, with her exploding and logging off in seething anger. I was never quite sure if she would return for the next. But then I was getting familiar with her pattern of apologizing after outbursts.

Over time I learned why. It was what I suspected: her passionate political execrations were followed by crashing depressions. It isn't uncommon with high-intensity clients. Intense emotional highs are followed by agonizingly black emotional lows. If she were capable of handling them without help, she would not be seeing psychological help in the first place.

I had not learned to expect that yet, however. So

that first time, I simply sat there stunned.

In my twenty plus years of clinical practice, I have encountered people running through every extreme of emotion. People ravaged by grief over the loss of loved ones; people heartbroken at sexual betrayals; people whose entire lives have crumbled with the loss of their jobs or businesses; people whose nerves have been shattered by drug usage; people so depressed at the meaninglessness of all they see that they may take their lives at any moment.

Years of training had steeled me for intensely dramatic responses to *personal* crises.

But I never imagined I would come across a client spitting with near-psychotic rage over municipal police funding policies, or falling into borderline suicidal depression over State voter ID requirements.

Even stranger was the way that Greta's politics, so full of apocalyptic drama, seemed to have completely swallowed up her *subjective life*. Her husband and her child seemed utterly forgotten. She might well soon lose her job—she was already endangering it by repeatedly calling in sick and not showing up, purely to spend the day 'organizing online.' Getting online to organize was more important to her than work. She showed me that she found her online life in online forums and communities supremely meaningful, immensely important—even though she had never met any of her comrades in person, never even knew their names, only their usernames and handles, never even attended an actual protest in the flesh out of fear of the pandemic.

I was startled by how her subjective life had become so completely consumed by politics, and yet by how that subjectivity was so completely exteriorized across the web. She was living in two worlds, the real and the virtual, but the real world, the one containing her husband and child and job, was withering away. She seemed to live entirely online. Her daily, tangible, physical, *personal* life had dropped off a cliff.

I felt as though I had encountered an entirely new psychological condition, a psychological situation, no one had ever seen before. I myself had never seen anything quite like it. It *seemed* to be a kind of addiction—an addiction to social media. It *seemed* to be delusional—except that Greta's delusional world was shared on multiple cult-like online forums in which thousands, perhaps millions, of people affirmed each other's picture of the world. It was not the ideology itself. Other, more right-wing individuals who shared bizarre conspiracy theories about 'Qanon' or Obama's birth certificate or Jews, congregated online in much the same way.

It resembled psychosis, but it was a shared, socially reinforced paranoia. Yet a socially reinforced psychosis that was not social at all, for Greta had not met one single person whom she had 'organized' in real life!

Just as disturbing was the deeply exacerbated hyperpolarization I was witnessing. Greta did not merely disagree with those on the other side of the political spectrum: she *hated* them, she *loathed* them, she *seethed*. I was seeing dehumanization of The Other on a profound scale, a dehumanization I feared could sink into psychosis. It was so over the top, I could not but suspect some completely different inner frustration as the root.

Greta's anger sought out despised human targets, enemies, to visit itself upon. A classic case of displaced aggression. But why should obsessive amounts of internet time deepen that anger, or foster such acid hatred?

What was going on? What exactly was I looking at?

Here I should pause a moment, just to be very clear:

Therapists are human beings like other human beings. They too have political opinions, religious opinions, social opinions. They may have strong preferences regarding the arts, or lifestyle choices, or sports, or items in the news.

All that is put to one side during the therapeutic conversation.

The therapist is there to *help the client*, not to persuade the client to share his or her views, and absolutely *not* to condemn the patient for any views that the patient may hold.

I don't want anyone to imagine, even remotely, that I was trying to argue Greta from one position into another, or that a therapy session should be a debate about political policy decisions. The task of a therapist is to heal, to empathize, to open a mindful psychological space for clients, not to advocate or attack any ideology or faith or worldview.

What concerned me about Greta was not her opinions, but the self-evident pain and depression she was experiencing, the distraction and isolation, the maladaptive thoughts and feelings and behavior that were visibly causing her harm.

That they *were* maladaptive was obvious. She was completely neglecting her child. She had no time for other activities or casual entertainment or going out. She was ignoring her husband (and adding to his own not inconsiderable stress and depression). She was just not there for anyone. Not even at work, where she was increasingly receiving warnings, because even *at* work she would be getting on social media.

Moreover, she was extremely sensitive to warnings and criticisms her managers were increasingly passing along to her. She ascribed them all to politics, and struck back. She felt herself surrounded by right wing enemies and complained about persecution to Human Resources. When the investigations turned up no indication of mistreatment, she accused human resources of sharing the same right-wing biases.

On those rare occasions when she needed to physically appear at the office, she would; then she'd rush to the company bathroom to watch CNN, MSNBC, PBS, on her Android, while at the same time her DVD player was taping the entire day so she could watch the same programs in the wee hours of the morning. She would get no more than two hours sleep a night for days at a time. If she drove somewhere in heavy speeding traffic, she'd text messages to her fellow Facebook activists regardless. And if a police cruiser took notice? That was additional proof of surveillance and repression and persecution.

Lack of sleep seemed to push her thinking to even further extremes. At first, she had blamed the government incompetence and failure to support universal health care for the spread of COVID. Soon she was suggesting that the disease was a form of bioterrorism designed to reduce the numbers of the poor and of marginalized communities. The pandemic was all a plot to erase People of Color off the face of the earth (while desecrating the earth for the benefit of the oil companies).

Greta would find confirmation in, of all things, Nostradamus: she became convinced that Nostradamus had predicted the pandemic and Trump. She was not a person of faith, but the End Times was not a metaphor to Greta. Collapse was imminent and apocalypse inevitable.

Morality and egocentricity melded in her in strange ways. She had a very inflated sense of herself and her moral worth. "I am a good person, a just person, I am doing the right thing, I am struggling for what is right and for a better world. I support the family, I pay the bills! *Who is my husband to criticize me?* Who is *anyone* to criticize me?" Yet assertions of her own goodness and high morality would spill out intertwined in the most acid demeaning of others.

More than once she admitted that she was on the point of asking her husband for a divorce. She looked down on her husband. He had lost his job.

He was a loser. But, worse than that, he said he *wasn't interested* in hearing the truth, he *didn't care* about the poor and oppressed.

"Doesn't he have a right to his own opinion?"

"*No!*"

"What if your husband had kept his job, and you had lost yours? Would he divorce you?"

She hesitated. She admitted the answer was no. But then immediately pivoted to Donald Trump. So much for the rest of the session!

I didn't confront her. Nor did I defend Trump. (On many points, who could?) That was not my job. The task of therapy is not political debate but emotional equanimity—the goal was to meet the client on the plane of lived experience, and to point to ways leading to a more open, less self-destructive, engagement with that person's individual circumstances. The client's political opinions may come along on that journey and be waiting intact at the end of that journey. But opinions should remain only opinions, borne lightly, not worn like chains. The place the client finally arrives should be a free space, not a prison.

There is nothing wrong with social activism as such. In fact, I found myself in agreement with Greta on more than a few of her points. But when you ignore your child and your spouse, or break with relatives and lifelong friends, or alienate coworkers or business associates; when the expression of your opinions is tinged with rage and followed by days of black depression; then something larger and darker is occurring which needs to be addressed.

In such cases politics has become a symptom. But in the case of Greta specifically, what was the underlying disease? I needed to scrape away the hard surface of her strident, exclusively political language to reach the personal issues underneath.

There remained a certain delicacy, a certain *nuance,* in how the therapist approaches clients drunk on ideology, in the grip of passionate opinion. For instance, one of the keys to successful therapy is empathy. How can the therapist achieve that with an extremist, whether on the left or right?

Often the same way that people in casual conversation do: by finding some common ground with the other person. Therapists who have similar educational backgrounds, or life histories, or ethnic backgrounds, or hobbies, or even political views, can sometimes establish a quicker or deeper connection than therapists and clients with considerable personal differences. Like harmonizes with like.

That doesn't mean that a therapist has to mirror the client in every way. But some shared characteristic can help bridge what I think of as 'empathic gaps': the client's feeling that the therapist cannot understand their situation. A therapist can always *imaginatively* empathize. But to intuit what the inner life of other people, different people, is like, is a learned practice. To actually have had the same experience is the royal road to fostering such a bond.

In the case of Greta, it was obvious that there

was actually very little connection between her views and the online manner of involvement with them that she had constructed. Her own politics might be explicitly leftist, but it was easy to imagine a right-wing client following the exact same pattern, visiting right-wing web site fourteen hours a day, organizing right-wing protests and fundraisers on dozens of right-wing groups and right-wing forums, ignoring wife and child and job and shouting down people who expressed other views. The *form* transcended the content.

As a cognitive-behavioral therapist, I found this both puzzling and intriguing. The content of her views, her cognitions, *seemed* to be driving her behavior. And yet in another sense they didn't, not at all. One could easily imagine the exact opposite of her opinions driving the same behaviors.

It was no small challenge. Typically, the cognitive-behavioral therapist will encourage a client to examine and critique their views. As thoughts change, behavior often changes too. But in this case, if she flipped from one political extreme to the other, she might well find herself acting in exactly the same way!

At the same time, I felt there was a path to a solution here. I had to stay away from content, and modify the form directly. How?

If I seem to be presenting a Greta with deep mental problems, it's unintentional. She most certainly *did* present paranoic and obsessive symptoms. Yet her story is one of quick and significant improvement, followed by a happy ending. In less than six months, she had put the worst of her condition behind her.

What did I do to help?

First of all, I did not debate politics with her. I repeatedly made it clear to her that my concern was with her, the *person*, and her personal, individual life. I did what I could to redirect her attention to the world of her direct immediate experience, *not* at her image of the outside world as filtered through social media.

"Greta, look around you," I would say. "Look at your life You still have your job. You still live in your home. Your child goes to school, your husband is highly qualified and is looking for a new position. You shop for groceries, you eat your dinner, you pay your bills. Yes, we are in a pandemic, and there are many things happening in the news. But how much has your *personal day-to-day life* really changed?"

She had to admit that, really, the only major change in her life was the amount of time she was spending on social media. Was looking at a computer screen for hours upon hours upon *hours* a positive change? Was it actually helping anyone?

I asked her to show me some evidence that her organizing was tangibly benefitting one single person. She couldn't. Were the staggering depressions that accompanied sleepless nights browsing social media a positive change? No.

Greta spoke a great deal about the importance of what she was doing with her online activities, and I pressed her on that opinion. Exactly what was she accomplishing? The whole of her political struggle seemed to amount to no more than talking online with people who held the same views as herself. How exactly did that 'save the world'?

Even what appeared to be a large contribution of her personal time was not so great, because she juggled too many causes to make any great difference to a single one. Anti-racism, BLM, LGBTQ, homophobia, transphobia, feminine empowerment, immigrant rights, she was involved with all these things and more. True, each gave her a sense of importance, of achievement. Each had online forums and message boards and social media hubs, and Greta belonged to dozens.

But what was she actually doing that produced any real concrete change in the world, other than holding scattered conversations all day long with others holding the same opinion?

I was not arguing with her views, or attacking them. On the contrary, I shared more than a few of her hopes and assumptions. I agreed—and still agree—that that social activism can be a good thing.

But what was she accomplishing in fourteen hours a day on Twitter that she couldn't accomplish in twelve? Or ten? Or seven? Was she accomplishing anything at all?

Greta told me she belonged to numerous activist groups online, organizing and meeting and developing outreach. She followed multiple news sites and services, and subscribed to updates that filled her email box each day. She connected almost daily with each one, and it simply left her with no time for anything else. She would push the software work she had to do late into the night, wrecking her sleep, and impairing the quality of her work. It resulted in a vicious circle of even more anxiety and depression. If I pointed out the self-destructive nature of such a way of life, she would answer that her important work, her *real* job, was fighting for social justice.

"How well can you fight for it if you're on anti-depressants while you're half-asleep? How much will you be able to contribute if you lose your job? Maybe *cutting down* on the number of hours you give to your political struggles is the best way to struggle more effectively. Better an hour of focused thoughtful activity than ten hours of unfocused rambling and web surfing."

The arguments began to sink in because they were not arguments: they were experiments, intended to lead her to be more sensitive to the palpable results of her actions.

For instance, I asked her to practice a Behavior Activation Model in which she had to regularly make herself aware of her compulsive habits of computer and phone usage and curb these behaviors. She was given a task: don't turn on the laptop or the phone first thing in the morning. Instead replace these rituals with other, healthier ones, like having a cup of coffee in calm silence, making breakfast, helping her son prepare for school, going for a Yoga or meditation class.

She made a morning chart each day in which she listed simple, positive, substantive activities that did not involve a computer screen. Reading a book. Listening to some favorite songs. Going for a half-hour walk.

She was fighting an addiction, and the goal was to replace a negative addictive substance with a positive one.

Change did't come immediately, but it came. In four weeks' time, Greta was becoming able to sleep better and began to connect with "real" people again. She participated in a cousin's wedding. She took a road trip to Wisconsin with her family. She revived an interest in gardening that she'd long put aside. She took a class at a learning annex in a new computer language. She and her husband began watching old Disney cartoons with their son.

Every item was a homework assignment that she and I worked out together, and every item chipped a half hour or so away from a day otherwise committed wholly to online politicking.

Soon she was calmer in her sessions, I began to see her laugh and relax.

Was I only trying to break unhelpful patterns? I was trying to do that, yes. But I also tried to remain sensitive to another issue: Greta's deep thirst for meaning. I gave her Viktor Frankl to read, so she could experience his own great response to historical injustice: surviving it, living on, living well, and using that life to be of service to others.

I suspected that, from what she told me about her relative powerlessness in childhood, Greta had developed a frustrated thirst for power. I tried to get her to see that it was most of all in her own life that she could truly exercise power. What could

she actually do that would affect the tragic historical fact of slavery, or of women not having the vote
till 1920? Nothing.

But she *could* see to it that her child was well fed
and well clothed, that the job she was doing which
supported the whole family was competently done
and not in danger owing to her neglect, that her
husband was helped in his job search instead of being hobbled by being demeaned and insulted.

In all these ways, she could make a direct concrete critical difference. A powerful impact on her
own life and that of the people most dear to her.

But if she never appeared on social media again,
would BLM collapse? Would the organization even
notice? It was not a matter of encouraging her to
stop her activism cold. She did not have to stop
supporting her causes to prioritize home, job, and
family. If her emotional life stabilized, she might
well become a better and more effective activist.

I asked Greta to record in some detail her actual
day—not her *virtual* day, but the real day in which
she interacted with people whom she did, after all,
love. How often did she talk in person to her husband, her child, her friends, her colleagues? When
we began, the answer was close to never. But
slowly, over several weeks' time, there began to
appear the diary of a life lived, not of web sites visited.

One of the things that had drawn Greta into the
political internet was the sense of drama, of *meaning*, that daily life tends to obscure. But it was not
that her daily life lacked meaning as such, only that

she had fallen into the habit of giving it no attention. Facebook had absorbed it all.

But meaning can be found wherever a person looks: and the more attention she gave to her husband and child, the more meaning she discovered.

The behavioral changes I suggested were small enough not to be resisted—a *gradual* increase in the number of hours spent sleep, a *gradual* lessening dependence on drugs and caffeine, *gradually* spending more time with her newly restarted passion for gardening, a *little* more time each day with her child and spouse. Small actions to take, but large in their collective impact.

No less important was challenging her core beliefs. Not her political beliefs, which I would not discuss, but rather her beliefs that her current activity was her only source of meaning.

Keeping the focus on her daily life offline would reveal the areas where she was truly facing challenges—in particular, job anxiety and depression. And that was where change really began. This gave her a chance to focus on and talk about *herself*, about what she wanted to change about herself, about her background, her struggles growing up, about personal things that mattered to her. The story she began thinking about was *her* story again, not the story of a battle between saints and devils and the end of the world. I was helping her re-establish her internal locus of control, helping her hold to it, and not give it up to narratives floating impersonally in cyberspace.

That doesn't mean her political outbursts didn't continue. Greta's appointment would begin and I would say, "Well, Greta, how is your relationship with your husband coming along?"

Her eyes would flash.

"There are *more important* things going on in the world than just *me*," she would bark. *"My life doesn't matter!"*

Here was a successful woman, blessed with a healthy child, a loving husband and a lucrative job at a time when hundreds of thousands of people were dying and the entire global economy seemed at the point of collapse. I found it strange to have to say to her,

"Yes, your life *does* matter. It matters to your famiy. It matters *to you*. It matters very much."

I found it strange to have to say that. But I didn't find it hard to say it. It was the truth.

At times I became quite blunt: "If social justice means so much to you, why don't you leave your family and quit your job. Why not riot in the street, attack police, and go make bombs?"

I asked the question because I wanted her to give me the answer I knew she felt in her more sober moments. She didn't *want* to hurt or attack others. She loved her family and wanted to be with them. That too was the truth. A truth she had too often left unspoken.

Week by week Greta began inching towards recovery—not recovery from her opinions, only recovery from holding those opinions in an obsessive isolation combined with continual immersion in online media.

Her slow reintroduction to the 'real world' was

accompanied by a gradual tapering off of her anxiety and sleep meds. When we finally parted ways, she was on the lowest dosage ever of her Lexapro (anti-depressant). In six months, she had made so much progress that there was no need for her to continue visiting.

I suppose I shouldn't have been so surprised. B. F. Skinner often said that one way to reduce a behavior was to replace it with a more reinforcing behavior. It's certainly more reinforcing to spend more time with family and with people you love and who love you than to follow Donald Trump online from morning to night. (Unless you *are* Donald Trump, I suppose.)

That applied to work too: the more time Greta had to give to her software contributions, the better her performance became, and the more positive comments her managers and colleagues gave her. The more compliments and talk of bonuses and promotion came her way, the less her managers seemed like fascist class enemies.

It was her experience of *actual life* that made this clear to her, however, not merely my arguments. The key wasn't to simply turn the computer off—that wasn't an option for a professional software consultant. The key was to reconnect her with real, tangible, lived experience and not, exclusively, virtual experience.

Greta's treatment worked out well. Even so, her case remains with me. I wouldn't say that it haunts me, exactly. But I can't quite let it go. Her condition is something I'd never encountered I suspect that it's more widespread than people know, and more likely to grow even more widespread than it is now. It could be reduced to its historical circumstances, of course. The coronavirus pandemic increased stress and anxiety for everyone. The lockdown forced people to stay at home, and as a result online usage soared. The 2020 election and the urban protests and rioting accompanying the pandemic fostered an atmosphere of extreme partisanship. In many ways Greta's condition was an illustration of the times.

But anxiety over viral infection remains, partisan division hasn't gone away, and obsessive internet use sometimes seems universal. How long has it been, Reader, since *you* were last online? Fifteen minutes? An hour?

More disturbing to me as a therapist was the way Greta seemed to have become totally absorbed in her virtual life, so absorbed that she seemed almost unaware of her real life and relationships.

Back in the 1970's, Marshall McLuhan, a philosopher of communications technology, wrote that in the electronic age human beings were becoming so immersed in media that physical life itself was falling away. The end result would be something he called 'Discarnate Man,' an intangible creature living completely in a hallucinatory world of pixels and data.

That day is not here yet, but Greta's experience was an unsettling presentiment.

What *distracts* you from your life diminishes your life. And there were moments when her son and husband and profession and her very self seemed to have dropped out of her mental space entirely as her online activism replaced them.

Just as unsettling was the realization that her 'dematerialization' into the web was not singular. With social media, if you have an idea, however crazy, you can immediately find hordes of people who have the same crazy idea. You're immediately welcomed into entire communities of the crazy, with news sites that supply crazy news items, and crazy PhDs and crazy think tanks that produce credible-looking studies that support your crazy idea.

And because in such communities the crazy idea is a commonplace, the brightest and most clever and most radical members of those communities will tend to push the crazy idea to even crazier but logical-seeming conclusions. Some of those advocates may not even be human at all: increasingly, some of the most active and passionate voices are not even human beings, but Artificial Intelligence mimicking and recycling those voices. We face the weird spectre of being drawn into autonomous social conversations between articulate machines with no consciousness at all.

Greta had escaped from that bubble of a pseudo-world. But how many were still trapped there?

For a moment I felt surrounded by these large invisible purveyors of madness, and the moment was disturbing. Are we seeing the beginning of a genuine widespread new mental health crisis? Possibly. But it's maddeningly elusive.

Politics is not a mental illness, and neither is social activism, and neither is the internet. In many respects these things are very good things, and we all benefit from them.

But there's something about the combination that *can* worsen day-to-day life and mental experience for some; and worsen it significantly for many.

Greta's story helped me to be better prepared to see this emerging problem, and to help those like her in the future. I'm not as happy to say that I expect to see more such cases in the future. I remain concerned—deeply concerned.

What exactly is our constant, ever-increasing, almost 24/7 immersion in social media, tweets, smartphones, the internet, interactive artificial intelligence, doing to us? To our mental health? Is our situation today, drowning in technology and ever-increasing technological innovation, helping to foster peace of mind and sanity, or is it generating a breeding ground for forms of mental crisis the likes of which we have never seen?

We have no idea. The case of Greta may be a harbinger.

## CHAPTER ELEVEN

# A PSYCHOLOGIST'S REFLECTIONS

## On The Therapeutic Life

"How you deal with all this, Dr. P? Doesn't it get to you? Hour after hour of pain and agony, sadness and tears? What gives you the strength to get through this?"

My clients sometimes ask me this. And I agree, yes, it's not an easy job. Of course every day is different. Some end with optimism, success and hope! But many days are heavy with frustration and despair. Films depict therapists wearing expensive suits as they sit in plush offices listening to cataracts of misery issuing hour after hour from intense but attractive movie stars lying next to them on The Couch. Meanwhile the therapist makes out his or her grocery list in the notebook.

How far from the reality!

What goes on in my mind when I see someone walk through the door to my office and struggle to open up, bare their pain, their secrets, their shame and helplessness, constantly saying *"I'm sorry, I'm so sorry... Why did I say that, why did I do that?... It's all my fault... I'm garbage, I'm worthless... Oh, God... Why did this have to happen?... Why can't things be different?... Why can't I be different..."*

Do I pity them? Certainly I feel for them. Very much so. Do I empathize, share those feelings, do I have to struggle hard at times to maintain my objectivity? Yes, I do. Do I want them to rise above their sufferings, their limitations? Of course I do. Do I feel powerful, smug, sitting there in that authoritative chair? I certainly don't!

My stories in this book offer a glimpse of my everyday life. And no, it is not a simple life, looking deeply into the lives of others. I walk in their shoes. I feel what my clients feel. What they have gone through in some cases has nearly destroyed them. I journey with them, but despair and self-destruction are not options for the therapist. I'm there to pull them out of the darkness, back from the brink. I offer my hand, but, just as importantly, my professional guidance and personal example. I have to model the sanity and stability that they fear and feel slipping away.

It's hard.

One of the subjects I took during my doctoral program was called, "Client-Centered and Experiential Psychology." We did role-playing. We would play client one day and clinician the next. As clients, we weren't scripted; we didn't perform made-up parts. We opened up about our own very real struggles and pains and hurtful experiences. We all found it cathartic. We didn't 'act' the role of client: we *were* clients during those sessions. Many of us broke into tears as we delved into our own unresolved issues.

That method, the experiential method, stuck with me. It shaped me in becoming a more empathic clinician, and it remains with me today. I don't embrace the pop therapy cliché of the therapist saying, "Yes, I know how that must make you feel." There is an arrogance, a presumption, in suggesting that you can know another person fully and completely and perfectly. But you *can* get an felt notion of what another person is going through. And you must.

I sometimes think that that capacity stems from a link between empathy and imagination. We cannot literally step into another person's shoes with their own feet, but we can *imagine* what it is like. We can gather data through observation, but once we do, we can go further, build on that data, and put ourselves into their situations intuitively in a way that preserves yet gives life to the data we have witnessed.

Stepping into my client's shoes helps me take that gathered information and step beyond it in a genuine, authentic manner. I relate to their agonies, their helplessness, rather than looking at the problem from an inauthentic distance coldly and externally. This helps me build a genuine connection with my client, a strong and trusting therapeutic alliance.

A *balanced* blend of empathy and direction helps me help my clients attain their goals. The surprising thing is that it has also helped me. I honestly believe that practicing psychology has helped me to be a better human being in my personal life, and changed my perspective on life for the better. Like the client, the therapist must strive constantly to be more patient, more kind, more sane, more wise and more real.

Clients do just that: they defeat their demons, and the therapist also follows in those footsteps. Each day I learn from my clients and at times, and often I will look at my own inner and outer life and ask how I would approach those situations from a supportive insightful psychologist's perspective. I certainly can't claim to be perfect, but do I believe that seeing and helping people strive and succeed to better themselves, learning from them, has made me a better person too? I do believe that.

Therapy redeems therapist as well as client.

What have I learned from my clients, and from the cases I've presented in this book? You the reader can draw your own conclusions from your reading, but after twenty-two years of providing therapy, I've drawn some conclusions too, and in this part of the book I would like to present them.

As I said at the start of the book, I would like people considering therapy to know something about the state of the therapeutic arts and sciences, and about which forms of therapy are presently considered stronger and more effective than others.

In the next section I'd like to talk about the

changing situation in regards to the causes of mental disturbances. In many respects we are in a paradoxical situation, practicing a psychology that has made rapid, indeed dazzling, developments and improvements and advances over the last few decades, while at the same time, mental health problems and issues are skyrocketing.

The title of a book by James Hillman and Michael Ventura says it all: "We've Had a Hundred Years of Psychotherapy—And the World's Getting Worse." That makes it sound like perhaps therapy itself is to blame, and nothing could be less true. Psychotherapy *itself* is definitely getting better and more effective, partly as a result of this very rise in public need.

Also, therapy is no longer stigmatized as once it was. Most people now believe, rightly, that there's nothing wrong at all about talking to someone to gain clarity, find solutions to personal problems, and lead a better life. That's simply the smart thing to do.

But as technique and effectiveness improve, and stigma declines, the ways in which the modern world fosters mental stress are all but exploding. Wars, substance abuse, fake news, pandemics, hyperinflation, hyperpolarization, behavioral addictions, economic uncertainly, seemingly endless crises—more and more people feel as though they are reaching the end of their rope, and statistics bear out this rise in mental stress, just as the newspapers give us daily updates about ever new stressors. We have new and vastly more complicated mental health challenges now.

For that very reason, therapy is needed more than ever, and the role of the therapist has grown more critically important than ever. I conclude with a section on how therapists can best deal with this changing situation, on where the profession may be headed, and some thoughts about the experience of being a therapist in these strange and difficult times—as well as its tremendous value, and its personal rewards.

## Current Trends in Therapy

Viewed purely from the standpoint of effectiveness and availability, the therapeutic situation has never been better. There are more trained and qualified therapists than ever before. There's more social acceptance of therapy than there has ever been. The effectiveness of therapy has never been more strongly supported by sound independent studies, and those studies are clearly and increasingly separating the most effective kinds of therapy from the weaker kind.

Therapy today is stronger than it's ever been. Looking at it, you'd think society was on the verge of a Golden Age of inner peace, adjustment, and sanity.

The exact opposite is the case.

Mental illness, depression, anxiety, suicide, are exploding. Over fifty million Americans—over one in five—are estimated to be suffering some form of mental illness. [1] Nearly one in seven have a serious substance use disorder.[2] Nearly one in twenty are experiencing serious thoughts of suicide.[3] Rates of depression are the highest in recorded history.[4]

By any humane measure, the therapeutic situation is a disaster.

If therapy is getting so much better, why is the population getting so much worse? What accounts for this paradox? How can it be addressed? How can it be understood?

## *The Pandemic*

The leading cause of the most recent mental health crisis is obvious: COVID. There's no need to explain why. We all saw the numbers of the dead and dying reach into the millions, we all went through the social distancing, the lockdowns, the masks. The fear and apprehension, the stress and changes that the pandemic brought, are part of our personal story as well as a matter of our collective history.

But the story of COVID is larger than that. Millions died of COVID, but billions experienced the stress and depression that COVID produced and that its aftereffects still produce.

In many respects the COVID years were almost an experimental model for how societies can generate and foster mental illness. The illness itself was bad enough. (Depression rates tripled during the pandemic.[5]) But the 24/7 apocalyptic pronouncements from politicians, the press, and the pundits, the avalanche of conspiratorial theories permeating social media—all of it drove a mass panic and despair that scars us even now.

Should we be thankful that the worst seems over? The statistics say otherwise. Yes, rates of depression tripled during the pandemic—but now that the worst of the pandemic appears to be past, the numbers on depression are even worse![6]

Judging by news reports, chronic paranoia is the new normal, and while the danger of infection may have (momentarily) abated, new stressors flourish. War in Ukraine. Hyperinflation. Massive job cuts and layoffs. Rising levels of crime. Exploding rates of divorce. Thermonuclear brinksmanship. Talk of civil war. Climate disasters. Political instability.

The pandemic alone is by no means the only factor now exacerbating mental illness. It's as though COVID opened a Pandora's Box of terrifying new stressors.

## A Therapist's Note On The Pandemic

How should a therapist face such an overwhelming situation? The question isn't an abstract one. There will almost certainly be future pandemics. If there has been any benefit at all to the COVID pandemic, it has at least taught up to be more prepared for what may come.

I can only speak of my personal experience. There were many firsts for me during the pandemic. The pandemic put an end to my normal clinical practice, at least as I normally practiced it. It also added a first to my twenty-plus years of practice: my very first personal burn-out!

The pandemic gave me a new identity—I became an 'Essential Worker.' My clients were instructed by the authorities to stay home, and 'socially distance,' and never leave their doors. They complied, and I supported them at the time. It was safer for them, we thought, simply not to show up at the office.

It's not that they wanted to discontinue therapy—the need was never greater. What changed was the way they received therapy. Instead of showing up face-to-face, they shifted *en masse* to digital technology. There were instant Zoom-like telehealth portals available almost overnight for consultations, and they were reliable and HIPAA compliant. Technology rocks!

But there were clinician's hiccups for me. I was trained to practice in person, in a confidential space, providing my client with a sense of safety and trust. Therapy is most effective in a personal encounter.

In person, the therapist can follow a client's body language and see their posture and how they hold themselves. Their facial expressions and intonation have a direct character in person that the distortions of a computer screen and speaker can't quite capture. When someone is present in person, they present any number of clues to that client's state of mind, to the level of their burdens, the truth or deception of what they're telling you.

That's not the case over a telemedicine platform. The clients' bodies are cut away. They become talking heads, shrunken heads seen at a strange angle, their voices intermittently inter-rupted or garbled. The most intense confessional moments may freeze owing to a bad connection.

But that was the only option. A much-needed option to help my clients get over the severe situa-tional anxiety and through the depression phase. The number of people who were anxious and de-pressed and in need of therapy exploded. I worked day and night, handling fifteen clients at a stretch at times. I felt morally obligated to do so, to tend to my clients, their irrational fear, their phobic isola-tion, their suicidal thoughts, all so terribly exacer-bated by pandemic conditions. The home lock-downs also led to newly acquired food and social media addictions, and to overindulgence in sub-stance abuse and sleep aids.

Telemedicine was not always easy for clients, either. Some clients had difficulty finding a private corner in the closet or bathroom of their tiny apartments, in their cars, or on a park bench. They couldn't prevent their pain from appearing in their eyes and expressions even in public places. I'm not sure how we manage to maintain privacy with children peeking into sessions, dogs barking in the background, and partners eavesdropping. Couples therapy is not a pleasant sight when it's two faces on one screen at times screaming and shouting.

It was a learning experience for me to digitally connect with my client, and a frustrating one. I couldn't pass them a tissue box when they sobbed on the screen. I couldn't give my older clients the comfort of a pat on their back.

Each day after my incessant virtual sessions, I

would rub my weary eyes, and go for a walk later in the evening feeling empty and ineffective. It was jarring and disturbing, personally and professionally.

I began to question my own competence, and sensed a growing exhaustion. I craved for a long break, to go away and be with my mother in India, where there was comfort and love and laughter.

But I couldn't. There were no flights. And then the pandemic began raging through India too. It was a scary and helpless feeling, with no end in sight. But then how could I counsel others about anxiety if I couldn't deal with my own? I held myself together, gave my attention to I taking care of myself and my nutrition, getting enough sleep and taking long walks. It helped.

Finally, in March of 2021, I was able to take a month's sabbatical and visit my homeland and my mom. That saved me from giving up my profession and my passion for being a clinician.

The havoc the pandemic wreaked on the human body is a matter of record, but I am convinced that the lasting damage it caused is the damage to our minds. "The door to happiness opens outward," wrote the Danish philosopher Kierkegaard, but the pandemic drove us all inward. During COVID-19, our doors were closed and barred. For once the masks we wore were not our everyday faces, but blank anonymity. The pandemic changed how we related to one another, and, like a stain in a cloth, the stain remains with us still.

But the pandemic had corollary effects, a psychological fallout. It exacerbated another dire aspect of the current therapeutic situation—an accelerated, exaggerated polarization.

## *Hyperpolarization*

One would imagine that mass illness, which is nonpolitical and nondenominational, would unify people, bring them together in the face of a common and impersonal enemy.

That didn't happen. There was already a growing division and polarization in society, a lack of common identity and mutual trust. The pandemic aggravated that trend, and dressed it in political language.

Pro-vaccine? You must be a Woke Democrat—a cultural Marxist! Vaccine skeptic? You must be a right-wing Republican—a fascist and a racist!

Russian or Ukrainian, liberal or conservative, man or woman, black or white, each group seemed to be pulling farther and farther away from its perceived enemies, dehumanizing its Other. Even with the pandemic now receding, the animosity continues, even deepens. Why?

A large part of the answer, surely, is social media. Just as our distant ancestors lived in small homogenous tribes, so we too have come to live in small homogenous tribes, but tribes of mind.

The liberal goes exclusively to liberal news sites to read only liberal commentary painting a liberal interpretation of the world, and the conservative goes to conservative sources for a conservative framework. Each informational bubble gives immediate emotional satisfactions, and each rests on fear, for neither is entirely real and both may pop at any moment. Many of us now live inside a sort of waking delusion, but a delusion underwritten by partisan news and a chorus of social media.

But invariably these subjective collective 'realities' brush up against objective reality. With painful results. 'Trump Derangement Syndrome' may have begun as a joke, but when marriages break up because one partner is pro-Trump and the other is not, or when a client gloats over assassination fantasies, it stops being funny.

### Political Therapy?

Again, this puts the therapist in a novel and difficult situation. Clearly a sort of 'political therapy' is needed, but it's not the job of a therapist to privilege one political philosophy or figure over another.

In my own experience with a hyper-politicized client, I sought to redirect the client's attention to the tangible facts of daily life. Are the dishes washed? The children fed? The bills paid on time? The problems of society seem titanic, but the problems of one single person are workably specific: all one needs to do is gradually direct the patient away from obsessive continual mental focus on some political object and onto those elements of direct experience that make life meaningful, worthwhile, joyful.

This is not to disparage activism. Fighting patriarchy or racism is well and good, but a decently prepared meal is good too, and if you don't eat at all you won't have the strength to fight anything. Having strong opinions is fine. Letting strong opinions have you is not. Speaking up is good. Speaking up courteously and intelligently, while being ready to listen tolerantly to opposing views, is even better.

Yet that sort of moderate partisanship seems rarer and rarer, and harder and harder to achieve. The hyper-partisan stance of political obsessives nowadays is strangely jarring, jarring because of its aggressive moralism.

To the hyper-partisan activist, left or right, those on the other side are not simply mistaken, but *evil*. One's political opponents are not merely wrong, but *Hitler.*

Emotionally, the realms of pure good and absolute evil seem to have been transferred from the religious to the political. And this is a novel challenge for the therapist operating in a hyperpolitical time, for the cognitive therapist is not there to tamper with the substance of a client's beliefs, only to guard the client from allowing those beliefs to be held with consuming, overwhelming destructiveness. The therapist has to deal with the problem of fanaticism using the tools of nuance. It requires considerable art.

*Unknown Ground*

The therapist today is challenged by more than political divisiveness among the client population. That divisiveness—in the form of political correct-ness—has begun to inform professional organiza-tions and standard practices as well. 'Misgender-ing' was not even a word a short while back. Now it's a punishable offense. What was deemed a mental illness by the DSM a few years ago is now considered a lifestyle choice to be celebrated.

The velocity of social change is such that it can leave the therapist seriously hampered. If a hus-band and wife, for instance, are having conflicts, a therapist can access entire libraries filled with books and studies on this perennial problem. Each couple is unique, but nonetheless one can find extensive descriptions of the standard interpersonal dynamics of couples. There are considerable accounts of practical experience detailing what sorts of therapeutic approaches are, statistically, the sort most likely to help.

But what if the husband is a biological female who identifies as a male, and the wife is a biological male who identifies as a female? It's not quite the same sort of relationship.

More to the point, it's not a relationship with a long track record in the psychological literature—or any track record. The therapist has to operate on new and unknown ground.

We can fairly assume that most anger management techniques will work well with whatever gender a client may identify. Straight, nonbinary, or genderfluid, anger is anger, and a slow deep breath is a slow deep breath.

But when even the researchers post articles online and in established journals informing us that there are eighty-one different genders and gender identities, even liberal therapists may find themselves falling into operational confusion. It's not that therapy can't help even in completely un-precedented cases; it's that the therapist no longer has the support of tested precedents; he or she (or *xe* or *xir*) is no longer sure what is most likely to help.

Also, it becomes more difficult to attain what I consider the Holy Grail of therapeutic practice, namely what I call 'attunement.' Effective thera-pists strive for an empathic identification with their client. They cultivate the capacity to intui-tively and deeply understand that client from that client's own perspective—to approach, even while maintaining their own personal integrity, the par-adox of a mutual oneness.

It's a goal that's far easier if the therapist and the client have some existing similarities. As a woman, I am already to a degree 'in tune' with an-other woman. As a wife, I can understand many of the experiences and pressures involved in being a wife. As an immigrant, I share with immigrant cli-ents (including male immigrant clients) an exis-tential knowledge about the stresses and para-doxes of living in a new culture.

But what does it mean to be a nonbinary post-cis Furry genderfluid Two-Spirit incel? It's a psychological perspective I personally have not experienced from the inside. I'm not sure that any working therapist has.

That doesn't mean that a nonbinary post-cis Furry genderfluid Two-Sprit incel couldn't benefit from therapy.

(I suspect that those of my radical behavior-ist colleagues, inclined to brush sciousness away along with all subjectivity, may be able to do so most easily. By giving their focus to measurable behavior only, they 'solve' the problem by ignoring the thoughts and feelings of those having them!)

Therapists like myself, who are concerned with a person's thoughts and feelings, however, encounter a wall that is difficult to scale. To attune oneself to a client always involves a certain active stretch of imaginative empathy, and there is only so far that one's imagination can successfully stretch.

Where there is only incomprehension, only an imaginative opacity, treatment can't successfully proceed. This is why I feel that there should always a preliminary meeting between therapists and clients. It can show whether the possibility of attunement is there.

When self-identification is without limit, and when the gulf between therapist and client is that large, is it still possible? Time will tell.

*Immigration As The New Human Condition*

There's another aspect of the current situation that's become paradoxical for today's therapist, and that touches on a subject rather dear to me.

In many ways, my career as a psychologist began with my thesis on immigration. Looking back, it amazes me how less complicated the situation seemed then.

Only a few years ago, an immigrant was a person who traveled from one culture to another culture, where he or she would experience the psy-chological pressures that were part of the process of adjustment.

How similar, yet how suddenly different, is the situation of the immigrant today! As America (and not only America) becomes ever more multicultural, immigrants find themselves in a new location, but not really a new country: rather, they find themselves in a new multicultural location without a single majority culture to which to adapt. Should the new American citizen speak English or Spanish? Should they speak in the accents of Woke culture or retro culture? Should they adopt the mores of the suburbs, of rural America, of Silicon Valley, of the hood? To which culture does one adjust when there are as many cultures as there are Cable channels?

The rise of multiculturalism has also fostered the rise of large persisting subcultures in the destination country, subcultures that stem from the immigrant's nation of origin, but just as often become variants. I'm thinking of my own Indian culture, whose American transplant bears such a heavy emphasis on professional eminence and material success. There are Indians in India with a similar material focus, but there it's not a defining national universal. Here, in my opinion, it's become an indelible mark.

This new Indian-American culture is not mainland Indian culture, nor is it quite standard American culture. Which culture then should the new immigrant from India acknowledge? To which should he adjust? And is it even possible to adjust when the speed of change is so rapid, and communications so increasingly universal? Multiple cultures are now everywhere: in India as in every other nation, American products, American media, American pop stars, American news, surround you even in one's national homeland. The Ukraine, Israel, Palestine, Africa, the EU, are all in the news wherever you are.

Immigration has become part of the human condition. We are all immigrants now, even if we stay in the same place, because our surroundings change so rapidly the accumulating differences make even the everyday seem increasingly foreign. We are seemingly always at home, and yet at the same time homeless.

I remember once hearing it said that the future is a foreign country into which we are all continually being deported. That saying has never left me. Adjustment to a new and stable social environment is certainly possible, and therapy can assuredly help with the psychological transition.

Constant 'deportation,' however, is an entirely different psychological state. One is not adapting to a new and fixed culture, rather one is being asked to develop the mental skills needed to cope with a shifting scenery of continual change. Therapy can help there too, but only a different sort of therapy, with very different goals.

### Sicknesses of Affluence

My experiences with immigrant communities in America led me to yet another paradox of the current situation: the strange proliferation of sicknesses of affluence.

Famously, the great Abraham Maslow posited a "hierarchy of needs," a theory of psychological health that suggested that basic human needs had to be fulfilled before full, healthy self-actualization could be achieved. Once one has food, shelter, clothing, stability, security, then one can and will look beyond, and strive to satisfy the higher needs of mind and spirit.

I've found that to be almost the opposite of the case.

Many of my clients are affluent. Very affluent. They have completely satisfied their basic needs. They're rich in every material sense of the word. Have they gone on to explore the needs of the mind on the wings of the spirit? In some cases. But for the most part, they are as rife with neurosis as any group I have treated—indeed, more so.

It's been said that the financially challenged cannot afford neurosis. (They can't avoid trauma, either, though they often have little choice, but that's another issue.)

The affluent, by contrast, are not only able afford to neuroses, they can afford to nurture and cultivate them. Perhaps that's part of the problem. Their finances allow them so many more options: drugs, divorce, political activism, sexual eccentricities. The wealthy have a much greater capacity to abuse reinforcing pleasures of all sorts, and rare are the individuals who can discipline themselves against all possible indulgences.

Many of those who can't discipline themselves, and go on to indulge in therapy. They too are a problem. There's nothing wrong in using therapy as a tool for exploring the self, of course, and many clients (particularly those given to psychoanalytic approaches) find a good deal of value over many years of self-examination.

Still, it disturbs me that wealth and affluence, freedom from the severe monetary constrictions and worries that so many face, should lead not to more personal satisfaction, but less. Sages have told us since time immemorial that money can't satisfy the needs of the soul, but therapists should be aware that, as we become financially wealthier, we don't necessarily become mentally or spiritually healthier. On the contrary, we may find ourselves encountering new sources of stress, and greater opportunities for addiction.

Wealth gives greater freedom, but the question then becomes, what do we want to do with that freedom? Business leaders who've earned their wealth through hard sweat tend to repeat their habits of obsessive workaholism, but find no joy.

Those born into wealth tend to drift off into corrosive dissolution. Both sorts show up in therapy, in surprisingly large numbers, searching not so much for happiness as for an inarticulate longing for greater meaning.

Can therapy provide it? Based on my own experience—and certainly in the work of figures like Viktor Frankl—I'm confident that the answer is yes. Self-examination, in and of itself, is not philosophy, but deep enough self-examination brings the client face-to-face with larger questions than the self. These are some of the most satisfying of cases, and perhaps Maslow is correct that those who have fulfilled their most basic needs are ready for such flights.

But my therapeutic experience has shown me all too many cases where such people crash quite as easily to the ground. It is not only the poor that merit our compassion.

## What Is to Be Done?

As I said at the start: by every measure, our collective mental health appears to getting worse and worse. I sketched some of the features of the current situation, but what are the causes? What is the solution?

I certainly don't have an answer for all the challenges of a technological society, or of increasing globalism, or of an ever-quickening pace of revolutionary change.

But then I am addressing not society in general:

I am addressing you—the individual. I have no doubt that therapy has positive effects on society as a whole. But the individual client is its focus, and cognitive therapy can provide solutions and improvements in the situation for every individual whatever the situation. We may indeed live in a society that fosters mental illness, but we can take steps that protect us from its worse effects.

The first steps are simple. I nearly always recommend that clients (after consultation) reduce the number of medications that they take, including the over-the-counter and particularly illegal medications.

Exercise, diet, fresh air—all these do as much good for the mind and emotions as they do for the body.

I've come to regard social media and online experience in general as one of the very greatest contributors to present-day mental stress. So, I strongly recommend that clients learn to limit the time they spend online. One may have to spend hours online at work, but no one needs to spend fourteen hours a day on Facebook. Or Twitter or 'X' or the Drudge Report or 4chan.

Just as we should all carefully and mindfully plan our meals, we should carefully and mindfully plan our online diet. An online diet is not the same thing as online starvation—we don't have to stay offline completely. We simply need to use our time online sparingly, to set a limit to the amount of time we spend online, to the number of websites we peruse, and to the amount of time we respond daily to email.

Think before you log on.

And just as importantly, log off. Make time to connect to the real world now and then—take a walk down the street, sit in the park, look at the sky and the trees.

We inhabit an actual physical world, and playing with a pet or planting a seed or washing the dishes can be more than a simple exercise in mindfulness. More even than therapeutic. It can actually be a pleasure.

The digital world is addictive. It inclines us towards isolation from direct human contact, it addicts us to sounds and images, fantasies and events, narratives true and false, real and unreal.

The message of mindfulness through CBT leads us away from a mindless immersion in practices and media in which self-awareness drowns. It teaches us to give greater attention to our own thoughts and behaviors, so as to better navigate the real world and the real lives which we live.

*Can* we live better lives, even under the growing barrage of change that the modern world presents?

Not without effort, not without thought, and not without connecting meaningfully with others.

But yes, we can.

### On Being and Becoming a Therapist

In the prologue to one of his novels, *Lying On The Couch*, Dr. Irvin Yalom describes his therapist narrator thus:

*Ernest loved being a psychotherapist. Day after day his patients invited him into the most intimate chambers of their lives. Day after day he comforted them, cared for them, eased their despair. And in return, he was admired and cherished. And paid as well, though, Ernest often thought, if he didn't need the money, he would do psychotherapy for nothing.*

*Lucky is he who loves his work. Ernest felt lucky, all right. More than lucky. Blessed. He was a man who had found his calling—a man who could say, I am precisely where I belong, at the vortex of my talents, my interests, my passions.*

*Ernest was not a religious man. But when he opened his appointment book every morning and saw the names of the eight or nine dear people with whom he would spend his day, he was overcome with a feeling that he could only describe as religious. At these times he had the deepest desire to give thanks—to someone, to something—for having led him to his calling."*

Admiring readers of Dr. Yalom—and I am one—will find themselves flabbergasted by those opening paragraphs, for Yalom has elsewhere penned some of the most acid portraits of clients in the entire literature.

And yet, once the initial surprise is over, what can I do but agree with that passage? How very *true* those words are. Therapy is a *wonderful* profession. People come to you in pain and sorrow and slowly you see them get better, grow stronger, overcome their suffering, rebuild their lives and their relationships.

What more valuable, meaningful, sound and solid profession could there possibly be?

Am I happy that I embarked on therapy as a career? I could not be happier. Would I recommend it as a career to others? Yes. Absolutely.

The Greek legends say: Know Thyself. Helping others to know themselves is one of the most rewarding professions possible.

More than that: it is one of the most entertaining. We human beings have an innate love and need for stories, and therapy abounds in stories dramatic, ironic, heroic, thought-provoking, tragic and outright comic. I've shared ten, but I could have shared hundreds.

There are moments in therapy that are truly hilarious. I remember one husband and wife in couples therapy:

"How do you feel about women, Mr. Smith?"

"With my fingers."

"And you Mrs. Smith, how do you see your husband?"

"Ideally? On chinaware. Crisply sautéed, with a dash of white pepper."

How does one keep a straight face? Therapy can make you laugh, make you weep, and perhaps most of all make you think. Stories that would inspire a Dostoyevsky or a Proust walk into your office every day, and pay you for the privilege of hearing them. Few professions are more philosophical. Few professions are more insightful, and insightful in a very special way. For the therapist's most challenging client *is* the therapist. Helping others know themselves, examine themselves, re-shape themselves, is a daily exercise in applying those approaches to oneself.

I lead a happy and satisfying life, and I don't think I could have led it as well if I had not learned to carefully examine my own thinking, to personally act with greater mindfulness, to consider my behavior and decisions more responsibly, to face my emotions more honestly, and to better hold them in check when called for.

Experiencing therapy is learning to think and act in a better way, and providing therapy is a masterclass in learning to apply those techniques to oneself. I don't say that I've achieved personal perfection. Far from it! I do say that a person who spends a lifetime helping people improve themselves helps that person improve too.

The average therapist is not a Stoic sage, but I truly believe that those who take up the profession have taken up a path that makes it easier for one to personally flourish. It is not only the client who benefits from therapy.

Times have rarely been so stressful or so unstable or so rife in conditions that threaten mental health. There is a massive need for therapy and for additional therapists, especially for trained and qualified therapists.

It's my hope that this book inspires those considering a career in therapy to join us in this wonderful and meaningful profession. I made that choice, and I have no regrets. It has been a grand journey, and I would take it again, happily.

It's also my hope that this book inspires those

who may be considering therapy to take the next step and call a qualified practitioner.

Therapy works. Your burden can be lightened Not in all cases, perhaps, not instantly, and not without effort. But in many, *many* cases deep personal problems can be resolved; and in nearly all cases they can to some extent be alleviated.

It is not necessary to suffer. Things are not hopeless. You are not alone. There is help. And there are people ready to provide it.

# ABOUT THE AUTHOR

Dr. Rashmi Pandey is a Clinical psychologist practicing in Chicago, Illinois for over twenty-two years. She is a Chicago resident and practices psychology with an eclectic integrative style utilizing Cognitive-Behavioral Therapy (CBT), Dialectical Behavior Therapy (DBT), and a client-centered, experiential approach influenced by psychologists ranging from Carl Rogers to Aaron Beck.

Dr. Pandey received her doctorate in Psychology from the Illinois School of Professional Psychology, and trained at Alexian Brothers Behavioral Health Hospital, Vista St. Therese Medical Center, and Lakeshore Hospital.

Dr. Pandey initially worked in an inpatient hospital setting, treating trauma and crisis patients, and then made a gradual transition to independent practice. She has been an active researcher in the field of eating disorders and acculturative stress and has presented and published in these areas.

In *Attuned*, Dr Pandey shares what she has learned and practiced as a clinical psychologist while working in multiple treatment settings, helping those with debilitating depression, childhood trauma, drug and alcohol dependency, eating disorders, body dysmorphia, acculturative stress, couples and relationship issues, and internet and social media addiction, while striving to restore her clients' resilience and positivity through greater insight, self-awareness and mindfulness.

The compilation of real-life situations in her book *Attuned* gives voice to her practicing method, her reflections, and her wisdom.

Made in the USA
Monee, IL
02 May 2024